Perfect Phrases for Documenting Employee Performance Problems

Other Books in the Perfect Phrases Series

Perfect Phrases for Documenting Employee Performance Problems

Anne Bruce

McGraw-Hill

New York   Chicago   San Francisco   Lisbon
London   Madrid   Mexico City   Milan   New Delhi
San Juan   Seoul   Singapore   Sydney   Toronto

The **McGraw·Hill** Companies

4 5 6 7 8 9 0   FGR/FGR   0 9 8 7 6

ISBN 0-07-145407-1

This is a *CWL Publishing Enterprises Book* produced for McGraw-Hill by CWL Publishing Enterprises, Inc., Madison, WI, www.cwlpub.com.

 This book is printed on recycled, acid-free paper containing a minimum of 50% recycled, de-inked fiber.

McGraw-Hill books are available at special quantity discounts to use as premiums and sales promotions, or for use in corporate training programs. For more information, please write to the Director of Special Sales, Professional Publishing, McGraw-Hill, Two Penn Plaza, New York, NY 10121-2298. Or contact your local bookstore.

Contents

Contents

Contents

Preface

I firmly believe in a quote I once read by Dr. Maya Angelou that seems to fit the greater purpose of this book. The quote goes like this: *The area where we are the greatest is the area in which we inspire, encourage, and connect with another human being.* For me, this seems to sum up the reason not only for this book on perfect phrases for documenting employee problems but for all of the books available in this *Perfect Phrases* series.

This book is a communications tool for managers and leaders everywhere—a fast, easy-to-reference, real-world field guide to making positive behavioral changes in the workplace through the identification of a wide variety of performance challenges and then getting to their concise and straightforward documentation. This is done through a process sometimes referred to as *listing*, or *listmania*—the basic methods for crafting power phrases filled with short, focused expressions that are direct and to the point. Why is this process important? It is important because we live in a world with lots of rules, policies, and convoluted explanations—explanations that no one can understand, let alone really and truly care about. On top of this, managers today are being faced with breakneck-speed requirements at which to manage and lead, where fast and practical is the mantra and where ready-references for supervisors and managers at all levels is a much-needed and appreciated survival tool.

If you're a manager who wants to more effectively document performance issues and then follow up with helpful feedback, then this book is for you. *Perfect Phrases for Documenting Performance Problems* sets a positive and motivating example of how to document performance challenges in a quick, yet appropriate, written format. In addition, it offers reader-friendly tips and tools that I have gathered over decades of experience while working with the finest managers and leaders from some of the world's top organizations. You will find that all of these techniques help promote individual growth and learning, as well as personal and professional development in a turn-of-the-century workplace filled with tough challenges that can befall anyone.

Therefore, I am providing for you here a simple-to-follow, specific format for this book that I believe most managers and leaders will find extremely helpful. It also can be used as an ongoing and continuous management tool and field guide when the going gets rough. It is my hope that this book will assist you, no matter at what level you work within your organization, to successfully navigate the sometimes turbulent waters of employee performance and productivity. We work in a time where performance issues and employee problems are often unique, exhausting, and more challenging than ever for today's manager. How you choose to equip yourself to handle these challenges is what will separate you from the flock and move you and your employees forward in a positive and evolving direction.

I'm happy to know you'll be taking this book with you on the journey.

Anne Bruce

Acknowledgments

Once you have written more than a half dozen books, your family and friends seem to get used to your being behind closed doors. Neighbors stop looking for you in the front yard, while delivery drivers from FedEx, UPS, and DHL just instinctively know to leave a few dog biscuits for the dogs and all packages on the doorstep.

If there were a book called *Perfect Friends and Family*, I'd be the author. I have had so much support over these past 10 years since entering the publishing world. Everyone *gets it*—Anne's writing another book. I especially acknowledge my wonderful husband, David W. Thomley, also a great writer and creative and talented photographer, for all of his love and ongoing encouragement. And from the warmest place in my heart, I give special appreciation and thanks to my loving and magnificent daughter, Autumn Kelly Bruce. Thank you for always being in my cheering gallery, no matter what. While writing this book, together we planned your wedding and through it all you never stopped reminding me of how proud you are of my writing and speaking career. And to my sister, Rose Marie Trammell, thank you a million times for all of the

Acknowledgments

late-night conversations and words of wisdom that only a sister can provide. The graphics in this book would not have been possible without the design talents of my dear friend and colleague Elly Mixsell Shelswell-White. Thanks, Elly, for caring so much about my work and for always giving my seminar handouts and workbooks a creative and original flair!

To the awesome and talented team of editors and production staff at McGraw-Hill Publishing, you are the best—especially my Senior Editor Jeanne Glasser and Editorial Assistant Lara Murphy—two ladies who spin a lot of plates and never drop any of them! And to my friend and Senior Editing Supervisor, Janice Race, you make the production on my books an enjoyable and fun experience. It's always great to work with you! To the copy editors and book cover designers, you are the unsung heroes of the publishing world, and I thank you all for working your magic on this book.

And finally a big thank you to all of the people who make up my public speaking audiences around the globe, and to all of the seminar and workshop participants who keep coming back, bringing friends and buying books. Your heartfelt stories, e-mails, and letters continue to enrich my life by allowing me to be a part of yours.

Introduction

B y the time you finish reading this book, you will have gained a stronger handle and understanding on several clear-cut ways to document your employees' performance problems and more! Succinctly documenting what's happening in your organization is an effective communications tool that, when used appropriately, can help managers increase their organization's productivity and overall performance levels.

Will there be performance problems along the way, regardless of whether or not documentation is used? Count on it. Your employees are human, and humans make mistakes. The good news is, when we learn to document employee performance problems early on, by using specific perfect phrases, we save time, we get to the heart of the matter, and we have a much greater likelihood of helping someone recover from the problem and go on to do his or her best work.

I like the slogan of the manufacturer of the Saturn car—People First—because it speaks to the humanness of our work, our successes, and our foibles.

In this introduction to the book, you will be able to glean several helpful techniques and tips that will assist you in supporting and documenting perfect phrases in a variety of situations. This section of the book will set the tone for what's to come and show you how you can more effectively use this book to make a greater impact on the organization. Most important of all, it will illustrate how to help others to ultimately become their best and grow their potential.

Perfect Phrases for Documenting Employee Performance Problems is a comprehensive source to help stimulate peak performance and higher productivity in the workplace. Managers can only set clear lines of communication when they help employees to better understand how their jobs contribute directly to the objectives and goals of the organization as a whole.

How Organizations First Came to Document Performance Problems— Its Purpose and Its Peril

More than a half-century ago in the United States, a fascination developed among businesses to generate practices for doing annual or semiannual performance appraisals and reviews. The theory back then was that if a manager took the time to review the performance of an employee a few times a year, this would provide the manager a chance to point out areas of needed improvement. Thereby, the employee would be provided with an opportunity to learn and improve on her or his skills and overall performance. This is actually the way that documenting performance problems came to be in American businesses. Initially, this idea was a great one.

The purpose, at that time, of reviewing someone's performance was to help make that person better. And although that traditional theory is still practiced in many organizations worldwide, it has unraveled along the way. It falls far short of helping people to do better; instead, it makes them feel small or even humiliated.

In practice, annual ratings are a disease, annihilating long-term planning; demolishing teamwork, nourishing rivalry and politics, leaving people bitter, crushed and bruised, battered, desolate, despondent, unfit for work for weeks after receipt of rating, and unable to comprehend why they are inferior.
—W. Edwards Deming

So what's the answer to this dilemma? Dr. Maya Angelou says, "Now that we know better, we must do better." And the fact is, today most managers do know better—much better. And so for managers not to try and improve the system is a serious breach of employee trust and effort. It's taking the low road, not the high road, when it comes to developing human potential and helping employees to face and overcome their performance issues.

Reframing How We View Performance Documentation

How do managers improve a well-intentioned performance tool so that it works in today's twenty-first-century workplace? Managers can start by reframing the ways that they approach the entire process. It's all about coaching and developing people. It's not about judging, criticizing, and demeaning workers. The goal should never be to prod employees to become the best worker on the team. Rather, the goal should be to encourage all workers to continually grow, evolve, and improve themselves a step at a time and with a plan to map out a way to do it. Here's the most important point to remember: A manager who relies on evaluating talent annually via the traditional performance appraisal route is missing the key objective, which is to act first as a coach, not a judge.

Improvements in the process become almost impossible when a manager relies solely on using numbers to rank people. Numbers can never be an accurate representation of a person's ability or true talent. Numbers can only be representative of someone's ranking in a specific skill area of their development, but then can never accurately reflect the actual person. Even when a numbers ranking is used, those numbers should be self-assigned by the person, not by the manager. (See the Professional Development Self-Scoring Card Template in Appendix A.)

Whenever a manager assigns a number to rate a person's performance, that person is subject to feeling humiliated and degraded. The number assignment only serves to personalize that person's weaknesses instead of focusing on the true performance problems at hand. Besides, how can a behavior trait be changed through a scoring process? It can't. It's the organization's system that produces its behaviors, a subject that will be covered later in the Introduction.

It's *How* We Document and Constructively Relay Feedback That Counts

You've probably heard the saying, "It's not what you say, it's how you say it." Well both parts of that statement are true. What you say is important, and how you say it, or how you convey and document constructive feedback, is equally as important. Never document a performance problem without carefully reading and then reading again what you have put into writing. Have the words you've used been the best choices? Do they accurately describe what is going on with this person's performance issue? Could what you've documented be easily misconstrued? Is what you've documented specific and to the point, factual and not personal? Can what you have documented about an employee's performance problem be used as a starting point for building a plan to turn the problem around and build strength from weakness?

These questions quickly become a manager's litmus test for evaluating the perfect phrases he or she must find for documenting employee problems and other issues at hand. It also is a starting point for conveying fast feedback.

There's Nothing Like Fast Feedback When There's a Performance Problem Brewing

This book focuses on finding perfect phrases, and perfect phrases also include fast phrases—phrases that include helpful and constructive feedback in a hurry. Sometimes these phrases are referred to as *speedback*.

Feedback is best when it is frequent and immediate. By giving someone fast and immediate feedback, you will develop a number of fast-feedback phrases that you can use for documenting both good and troubling performance on the job.

Keep in mind that just about everything we learn to do well, or improve upon, we learn by receiving feedback from someone. Whether it's learning a new tennis serve or how to write a strategic business plan, we can all benefit from helpful and fast feedback in some way, shape, or form. In addition, when a manager takes time to give someone on-the-spot feedback, she is sending a powerful message. The message says, "I care about you and I want to help you to improve and to be your best."

Retired Army Captain Andy Mostovoj agrees. He is an experienced military leader and recent graduate of the Oxnard College Regional Fire Academy in Southern California and offers this metaphor: "Information of all types, especially feedback, is not like a fine wine—it does not get better with age." Mostovoj believes that it is always best to let people know when they are doing a good job shortly after they complete the job. He adds that, conversely, it is important that you tell them if they are performing poorly as soon as possible because you don't want people continuing down a path that perpetuates their mistakes—a good point that applies to all managers and leaders who care.

Take time to learn the five basic steps to delivering perfect feedback phrases.

Perfect and Fast Phrases for Effective Feedback

Step 1: Always Be Frequent and Sincere with Your Feedback

- Lois, I was just noticing that you were able to overcome all of the obstacles we discussed earlier last week. You're ready to go to the next step.
- Jeff, I know this isn't easy, but you can speed this process up by doing the following things first. Let me show you how.
- José, if you write these steps down now, you are more likely to remember them later. Trust me, there are too many details to keep track of in your head.
- Maurice, by speaking up and speaking louder, everyone in the group will better understand you and can give you more specific input on your ideas.

- I got your note Louis; this does sound frustrating. I am enclosing an article that I think will help and explain things more clearly.

Step 2: Make Feedback Fast and Action-Packed

- Hold everything, John. I like your enthusiasm, but you are moving way too fast for the team. If you just slow it down a bit, we'll all be able to keep up.
- I just received your e-mail, Linda, and I wanted you to know that all but point number 4 is right on target. Let's discuss that point now, if you have time.
- Mark, I can see by observing you today that you are frustrated. Have you tried asking Pete how he has done it in the past?
- Lee, you're not listing all the details of the project in your memos and so others on the team are missing important points. Please provide as many details as possible in your e-mails and memos from this point forward.
- Mohammed, I thought you'd appreciate knowing that you can actually skip this one step and still have the same outcome. I've learned it's a real time saver.
- Indira, you need to review all of the processes required before moving to the next stage of the project. I understand you are eager, but, believe me, your patience will pay off.

Step 3: Let Your Feedback Be Helpful and Corrective

- Justin, I don't think you realize how you are affecting others. You really need to think before you speak, to avoid hurting other team members' feelings. Did you notice the look on Sally's face this morning when you addressed her in front of the others?

- Sam, that's a shortcut that may have several safety risks. Let's discuss them one at a time.
- Laura, you've been struggling with this computer now for two days. I'd like you to partner with Mike today; he's a great coach on this particular system.
- Sara, I don't expect you to have all the answers this early on, but I do expect you to pay close attention to the details.
- Joan, you have a natural talent for this, but you need to master the technical aspects of the job first. Let's get you started.
- Let's meet as soon as possible, Mike, so that we can take a proactive approach to this particular performance problem.

Step 4: Be Empathetic and Sensitive to Others' Feelings

- I care about your learning this correctly, Martha. Let's plan to meet once a week for the next few months to go over your progress.
- Terri, you seem to be sensitive to criticism in this area. Please tell me how you would like me to provide you with the feedback you need on this.
- James, this may or may not apply to you, but I am going to share this with you anyway. What do you think? Am I missing anything?
- Bob, I have a strong feeling you are getting off on the wrong track. After I have explained this, I would like your input too.
- Jacob, please know I do not intend for this to be personal, but you have to understand our company's guidelines and customer concerns before you can go further.
- Jane, I understand why this might be so difficult for you. There are options we can discuss in the morning.

When asked, most employees will tell you that they welcome honest and even critical feedback, because they understand it will help them to improve and get better. The issue most people have is not with the feedback itself, but rather with the environment in which the feedback is presented and how that feedback is delivered. As a manager and leader, it is your responsibility to help establish a safe and respectful workplace for giving and receiving feedback of all kinds.

Step 5: Use Critical Feedback Phrases for Starters

Before you deliver feedback to someone, and in order that you may accurately document performance issues of all kinds, take time to set up these fast and perfect phrases to establish the feedback process:

- Phrase 1: Tell me how you would like to receive helpful and constructive feedback from me.
- Phrase 2: Share with me areas where you might be having difficulty or areas in which you would most like to receive feedback.
- Phrase 3: What would make you feel most comfortable when receiving corrective feedback from me?
- Phrase 4: Describe the best way that I can give you feedback as we move along on this project, such as e-mail, phone, face-to-face time, or meetings.
- Phrase 5: I can tell that you are extremely busy. How do you recommend I get feedback to you in a timely manner?

Feedback—It's a Two-Way Street

Documenting performance problems through use of effective feedback techniques and phrases can alter the course of a person's life, or the course of the work environment, moving workers toward taking greater initiative and improving performance. Your feedback, when it is done appropriately, can offer enormous, life-changing value to someone. But feedback is a two-way street that some managers forget to acknowledge.

The Receiving End of Feedback

Feedback isn't something we just give to others. Managers need to welcome feedback too. Feedback is, without a doubt, the best measuring tool managers have for determining their ongoing effectiveness.

When someone expresses his opinion or view on how leaders could have done something better, or points out something leaders may have neglected to do, it can be human nature to "bristle" a bit, or become defensive. But it's all about how you respond, not react, to the feedback that you get that makes all the difference.

Invite Feedback

Here are a few of the many benefits you'll receive as a manager by choosing to respond, rather than react, to the feedback you get from others:

- You will become empowered with the freedom to choose how you respond to feedback, thereby becoming more influential with your team.
- You will immediately benefit from others' perspectives and perceptions.
- You will make employees feel that their input is valuable to you.
- You can better focus on the positive points of feedback and not on the negative points.

■ You will begin to measure yourself against your own standards of performance and stop comparing yourself to what others are doing or have done in the past.

Think of feedback as a gift. When we choose to learn from the feedback we receive, whether it's positive or corrective, we can use the gift we've been given to improve the overall performance and productivity of the entire organization. But before performance is documented, it's a good idea to complete the following self-assessments.

Before Documenting Performance
Self-Assess on How You Give Feedback

Check your responses to the following:

	Usually	Sometimes	Rarely
I consistently provide others with constructive and helpful feedback.	☐	☐	☐
I use a variety of modes to provide my feedback to others, i.e. voice mail, face-to-face, e-mail, written.	☐	☐	☐
I take the time to diagnose or observe a situation carefully before giving my feedback.	☐	☐	☐
I take into consideration others' differences of opinion and views.	☐	☐	☐
I try to create an atmosphere of comfort when providing feedback to others.	☐	☐	☐
I first ask others how they would like me to provide them with feedback.	☐	☐	☐
Others never hesitate to give me feedback.	☐	☐	☐
When giving feedback, my approach is direct and honest.	☐	☐	☐

Assessment Explanation: If you answered "usually" to these statements, you are already using effective techniques that will help you to better document performance issues. If you answered "sometimes or rarely" to one or more of these questions, check with those who can explain how your present style of feedback is being received and how you might refine your style for greater impact.

Check your responses to the following:

	Usually	Sometimes	Never
I'm open to receiving feedback, both positive and corrective.	☐	☐	☐
I listen carefully and don't take critical comments personally.	☐	☐	☐
I thank those who provide me with any kind of feedback.	☐	☐	☐
I clarify and ask questions about the feedback I get so that I am sure to understand the message. I evaluate its content.	☐	☐	☐
I consider changing my behavior when I get corrective input.	☐	☐	☐
I do something with the feedback I receive.	☐	☐	☐

Assessment Explanation: Based on the responses you gave yourself, select the areas in which you need to improve, and commit yourself to those improvements.

Fast Phrases for Accepting and Receiving Feedback

Feedback is always best when it is...

- **clear and to the point**
- **based on work behavior, not personality**
- **specific**
- **objective**
- **job-related or performance-related**
- **based on facts**
- **solution-driven**

Why Documenting Performance Problems Is a Positive Step to Continuous Learning and Greater Opportunity

Anmarie Miller has held some of the most respected jobs at what has been called the most high-performing and profitable airline in the world—Southwest Airlines. She has facilitated performance training nationwide and has been an effective team leader in good times and tough times. Miller clearly sees the net result of documenting performance issues as both a positive step forward and a learning opportunity for all involved. According to Miller:

When there is a performance issue at stake, you really have to get to the bottom of things. Simply writing something down isn't enough to show you care as a leader. For example, maybe the task at hand has improved, like increased sales numbers, or less safety violations, but I believe a manager has to go beyond the obvious and continue to follow up with the person. To me, that means finding out certain things and asking pertinent questions, such as "What have you learned from this experience?" and, "What has helped you most to improve your performance at this specific task?" Once I've gotten a handle on these key points, I then emphasize to the person they are the one responsible for accomplishing the performance gain or improvement and that my role was to provide a safe environment for growing and learning, along with the necessary resources and tools for them to succeed. This method of communication has worked well for me, because it provides critical information necessary to lead and support and also builds the confidence of my team.

Later, in Part One of this book, we will discuss how performance problems can actually become an organization's strength finders, helping managers to better document employee problems early on using specific phrases and then providing employees with a plan to deal with those problems and eventually overcome them.

The Organization's System Produces People's Ultimate Behaviors

Earlier in this section, it was mentioned that the organization's system is what produces its people's behaviors. This point is important for managers to understand when they are preparing to document employees' behaviors, traits, and performance problems.

All organizations are systems, and likewise, your department, or team, is a system within a larger system. As in any system, the behavior of each of its parts affects the behavior of the system as a whole, which in turn affects each and every part of the system.

Managers, team leaders, and supervisors must be attentive to how all the various parts of the system are operating together and influencing one another. This is called having a *systems perspective*. With a systems perspective, you can begin to recognize that any single action taken can cause a ripple effect throughout the department, even the entire organization. Even a small mishandling of documentation of performance problems—incorrectly and nonspecifically—can easily affect the quality of your relationship with other employees. It can squelch motivation and a commitment to do better and learn over time.

Definition of Systems: Unified, multidimensional patterns found in human environments. The four parts that make up a system include inputs, processes, outputs, and feedback.

When managers understand that a business is a complex social and mechanical system, with dynamic connections among forces and patterns, they can begin to improve that system and make it better, more efficient, and more productive. During the process, the manager can positively influence employees' performance, behaviors, and motivation to do better. Thereby, they can work to minimize, or even alleviate, the

negative ways some people go about documenting performance issues by not providing support, follow-up, and a plan of
action as part of the system's process.

When *Pride of Ownership* Becomes the Perfect Phrase

A good on-the-job example of blending a systems approach
with effective on-the-job phrases that improve performance
comes from Eric O. Larson, team leader for Pediatric Transport
and Maintenance Coordinator of the Meducare Medical Transport Service at the Medical University of South Carolina (MUSC).
Larson says:

> Our employees are required to wash their ambulance
> each shift. Our ambulances are basically rolling bill-
> boards for our department and the hospital. I want the
> ambulances to be spotless and shiny. The crews are
> given all the products they need to make this [task] as
> easy as possible, like wash and wax soap and spray-on
> polishing products. However, as call volume increases,
> the staff has a hard time keeping the trucks as clean as
> I'd like them to be.
>
> Several months ago I sent out a department-wide
> e-mail titled "Pride of Ownership," which outlined rea-
> sons the ambulances should be kept in pristine condi-
> tion. The specific phrase I used in the e-mail that seemed
> to have the greatest impact said, "The cleanliness of your
> ambulance is not only a reflection of the department
> but also of you." I emphasized that it doesn't matter how
> pressed your shirt is or how much you have polished
> your boots. People who see you drive up in a filthy

ambulance will only remember how dirty your truck was.

Next, I assigned each shift an ambulance that they would always work out of and made it a contest. Every week I would inspect the fleet. The crew with the cleanest ambulance would be treated to lunch by the crew with the dirtiest ambulance. After the third week I started having five-way ties. We discontinued the "reward" because there was no one with the dirtiest truck to buy lunch!

It worked. The new system did produce people's ultimate behaviors. The employees now take pride in their clean ambulances. They are even complimented by other EMS departments. Now, if I ever notice a truck that could use a bath, I just walk through the day room and say the words, "Pride of ownership." The crews laugh a bit as they make their way to the wash rack.

Unlike Mr. Larson's approach, which is to create a more effective system for workers, many companies actually stifle performance by setting up unreasonable bureaucratic barriers. They may go so far as to attribute success or failure to the individuals involved while seeking to find flaws first. The problem with this situation is that those managers fail to recognize that sometimes performance is not under the direct control of the individual but often relies on the individual working well within the system created by management. As you move forward in this book, be sure to keep this important point in mind. What are you doing to contribute to, or contaminate, the system in which you work?

Part One

Indispensable Communications Tools

Beware of the Trauma You May Cause When Documenting Performance Problems

In the Introduction to this book, I discussed how and why organizations came to document performance issues in the first place—their initial good intentions and their eventual malfunction. The following story brings a real-world face to this critical issue and the importance of finding perfect phrases to document performance problems.

When a Single Word Without Explanation Won't Cut It

John, a supervisor at a well-known pharmaceutical firm, shared the following confidential story during an interview for this book:

> I remember when I was coming up through the ranks in this organization. I was eager, hardworking, and enthusiastic about the future until my manager documented my performance in a standard 90-day performance review.
>
> I distinctly recall that he wrote down in my file that my overall performance was "satisfactory." This one word leveled me. In my head, I was working so much harder and better than just satisfactory. What did he mean? Why wasn't the documentation more specific? Why didn't he

write, "John's performance was satisfactory based on his level of current experience"? That, I could have handled. Instead, I was simply labeled "satisfactory"—translation: lower than highly satisfactory, below good, and far below excellent or a job well done!

You may be thinking, why was this so traumatic? After all, my manager didn't write something terrible about me. But, you see, it was terrible. My enthusiasm was squelched and so was my confidence. The documentation without better understanding of what exactly "satisfactory" meant was insufficient feedback that took the air right out of my sails and slowed down my go-get-'em stride and positive attitude. That documentation haunted me for years, and I eventually left the department because of it.

John's point is well taken. As a manager, always be fully aware of the influence you may have over someone the moment you write down and document a performance issue. You don't have to write something derogatory to traumatize someone—one word can do it. Lack of specificity and ignoring a specific recommendation, or a way to help people improve their status, is enough to set them back and squash their self-confidence. So remember, it's not just what you say in your documentation that matters, it's also how you say it.

As you use these lists of perfect phrases for documenting performance problems, keep in mind that it will be up to you to provide a thorough explanation of the phrase suggested. A phrase alone is not enough when it comes to really wanting to help someone get better and reach his or her greater potential.

Let Performance Problems Be Your Organization's Strength Finders

Documenting an employee's performance problems is a delicate matter. When a leader takes the time to carefully craft what he is going to say about someone, that person helps to set the tone for future dialogue and ongoing improvement and personal growth.

Right now in some organization, somewhere, a manager or supervisor is meeting with an employee to discuss his or her performance problems. Some people would rather have a root canal! But they feel that way because managers and supervisors often focus on the problem and not on the strength that can come from addressing that problem head on. Leaders also fail to back it up by providing a method to somehow create strength in an otherwise weak performance. (See Appendix A, Sample Performance Builder.) We've learned from experience that the traditional performance appraisal, on its own, simply doesn't cut it.

So then how does one improve performance by focusing on strengths? It is done by developing better and stronger communications skills as a leader. When you document an employee's performance problems, you hold in your hand the power to affect that individual's long-term success and desire to change and evolve for the better. Documenting an employee's performance problems gives you, the leader, an opportunity to emphasize the vital qualities that that person possesses. You can also further elaborate on how that employee can transform those weaknesses one step at a time into something of greater value and meaning.

It is your communications skills—or the ability to phrase problems clearly, correctly, and effectively—that can remove the barriers to your employees' performance and productivity. When a leader does this well, she lets the employee know exactly where he stands and how far he needs to go to get to his best performance. That's the mission—continuous learning and growth, not criticism and ridicule.

Get to the Problem Sooner, Not Later

The key to communicating effectively and enabling continuous learning to occur is to identify possible problems before they happen, or as soon as they happen, not later, when irreversible damage may already have been created.

Performance communication is an ongoing process between a leader and his or her employees to ensure that performance challenges are identified early on, before they get out of hand and interfere with an employee's success.

The Process Begins

Documenting performance problems is an ongoing challenge when you want to bring an employee's performance up to an optimum level.

Doing so requires a process that should accomplish the following objectives:

1. Quickly identify and uncover obstacles to an employee's performance and success. Do this sooner, rather than later, whenever possible.
2. Help provide the person, as quickly as possible, with what she needs to eliminate those obstacles that stand in the way of improved performance and ongoing success.

3. Be honest and straightforward in your documentation. When you set clear expectations, you are preparing the employee—actually setting her up—for success rather than failure.

How you go about fostering the communication between you and your employees is up to you, but here are a few guidelines:

- Practice *management by walking around (MBWA)* and observing what is going on. Observation is the most underrated of all measurement tools. Plus, it's easy to do and cheap.
- Ask employees for ongoing status reports on projects. Don't wait six months to find out what is happening.
- Hold weekly meetings with employees to evaluate overall direction and review what has been accomplished to date.
- Provide lots of helpful and corrective feedback.
- Use one-on-one communication when a performance problem arises. Never ridicule anyone or point out someone's problems in front of others.

Review these communications processes with your team or workers. Then ask employees to share their specific techniques for doing a great job. It's also a good time to ask others to brainstorm their individual solutions to various performance issues. Oftentimes, other workers' tips, tools, and shortcuts can serve as valuable feedback for all concerned.

A key point is that basically there are two kinds of managers. One manager is dead set on making others feel small or lesser, so that he or she can feel bigger and more important. The other manager is committed to people first. That type of leader takes time to learn to communicate clearly and explain her or his actions so that others can learn and develop from that important and vital feedback. What kind of manager or leader are you?

Performance Problems: Strength Finders or Weapons of Human Destruction

Did you know that when you uncover performance problems in others and document them appropriately you also can use those problems as learning tools rather than weapons of human destruction? When we use performance problems as strength finders, we become capable of building a higher-performing workplace, a workplace filled with healthy morale, a strong work ethic, genuine effort, and a system that supports those efforts.

Perfect Phrases in Performance Areas Where Problems Are Most Common

A book like this could include literally hundreds of lists encompassing a wide range of performance areas. The lists in this section have been fine-tuned, however, to include the performance areas on the job where the problems and challenges employees regularly face most commonly occur. In other words, these are the areas you can be sure you will be dealing with most often and referring to most frequently.

How to Use These Lists

Remember, nothing is really perfect—even a so-called perfect phrase. The term itself, *perfect phrases*, is used to help you to document specific performance problems quickly, but they become even more effective when adapted and honed to fit your specific industry or management needs. Documenting anyone's performance problems isn't easy. It takes time and effort by both the manager and employee involved.

That documentation process is made a little easier by the lists provided throughout this book. You can quickly scan each list and then pluck out the parts that pertain to the specific situation at hand. By scrolling down each list under each category, you will no doubt be reminded of the problem areas you wish to face head on with that employee. I suggest using color markers to place checkmarks alongside a phrase in which you are particularly interested. Some managers and supervisors use red markers to check off entries or indicate a serious situation; others use blue or yellow, orange or green, to indicate increasing or decreasing levels of concern. Obviously, you are the best judge for indicating which phrases will best pertain to an employee's performance needs.

Above all, some of the things on these lists may actually help to stimulate employee/employer discussion and thinking. You'll want to use this book *before* you actually sit down with the person to discuss a performance problem. It's not something you pull out of your desk in front of the employee and reference with a highlighter!

Like it says in the Nordstrom employee handbook: Rule number one is to use your good judgment and common sense at all times. Rule number two is that there will be no other rules! We can all take a lesson from this kind of management wisdom. It is your good judgment and common sense used in tandem with the resources in this book that make these perfect phrases for documenting performance problems more than just words on paper. Rather, they will become vital tools for managing better.

Keep in mind that when documenting a person's performance problems, always be ready, when asked, to back up your documentation with specific examples. This preparation is critical. Next, have a plan of action to help that person learn from his or her mistakes and get on with a program for continuous learning and growth opportunities. Additional tools at the back of this book can help you.

If You Can't Back It Up, Don't Say It

The perfect phrases will allow you, the manager, the perfect opportunity to specify what you are referring to with action steps; you can then provide your own examples pertaining to that individual's performance challenges. Even a perfect phrase can't stand alone without the meaningful purpose and actions to back it up. That's your job. If you can't back it up, then don't bother saying it. And never overwhelm a person with the items on these lists. Select a handful of perfect phrases with which to start. The objective is to help employees to correct and learn from their mistakes, not to bury them in lists of weaknesses and performance failures.

In this next section, you will find perfect phrases for 30 of the following performance problem areas:

Communications Skills
Punctuality
Decision Making
Empowerment and Delegation
Technical Skill Development
People Skills and Relationship-Building
Coaching Others
Customer Care

Attitude
Handling Personal Problems
Creativity and Innovation
Meeting Deadlines
Leadership Skills
Negotiation Skills
Appearance
Self-Esteem and Confidence
Efficient Use of Time
Problem Solving and Conflict Resolution
Teamwork
Emotional Intelligence
Overall Productivity
Loyalty
Resistance to Change
Project Management
Safety
Goal Setting
Motivation and Morale Building
Common Sense and Good Judgment
Personal Growth and Development
Professional Growth and Intentional Learning

Communications Skills

- Needs to become an engaged listener, make eye contact, lean in, ask pertinent questions, and so on.
- Should be asking lots of questions to show interest and attention.
- Has limited attention span for people, needs to be expanded.
- Needs work in verbal skills.
- Has poor grammar.
- Needs to improve phone skills.
- Writes poorly.
- Spells poorly; too many errors.
- Mumbles.
- Needs to be articulate and compelling.
- Is too technical when explaining things to laypeople.
- Is weak when it comes to speaking persuasively and convincingly.
- Needs PowerPoint class.
- Could benefit from public speaking class, or Toastmasters.
- Has voice that is too monotonous.
- Uses body language that is not engaging or open to communication.
- Fumbles for answers; needs to think through responses.
- Comes across as defensive or threatened.
- Does not attempt to build rapport.
- Does not gain audience participation or involvement in presentations.
- Misunderstands others frequently.
- Would benefit from computer class for more effective and entertaining presentations.
- Expresses self well verbally but not on paper.

- Confuses people with both verbal and written communications.
- Uses e-mails inappropriately or writes poor e-mail messages.
- Rambles; memos need to be more concise and to the point.
- Needs to address business etiquette.
- Takes too long to make a point.
- Fails to take thorough notes for future preparation.
- Confuses others easily with convoluted terminology.
- Is sometimes difficult to understand because of heavy accent or language barriers.
- Has difficulty understanding others with accents but won't politely ask for clarification.
- Fails to have someone repeat the point being made to establish clearer understanding for both parties.
- Needs to summarize what has been said by others to be sure there is mutual understanding.
- Will not take time to spell check or grammar check proposals or other critical documents that represent the company.
- Is too casual in communicating with new clients.
- Needs to show more respect for older clients and senior leaders.

Punctuality

- Is consistently late.
- Shows up late for work at least once a week.
- Has used all sick days.
- Has used more than allotted sick days.
- Consistently calls in sick on Mondays and Fridays.
- Misses work and does not call in.
- Has a poor attendance record.
- Takes long breaks.
- Uses bad weather as an excuse not to show up for work.
- Very rarely comes back from lunch on time.
- Arrives late for meetings by at least 10 minutes every time.
- Clocks in late frequently.
- Does not recognize the inconsideration to others that poor punctuality brings with it.
- Does not understand it is rude to always be late or to not show up when others are expecting you and counting on you.
- Does not see the impact of tardiness on fellow workers.
- Is arrogant when asked about being late.
- Makes inappropriate jokes about not being on time.
- Needs to notify supervisor or manager of emergency absences as soon as possible.
- Should begin working within 10 minutes of arriving at work.
- Should start notifying someone if he or she is going to be late for work or a meeting.
- Needs to attend substance abuse meetings regularly, as agreed upon.
- Occasionally arrives at work under the influence.
- Needs to start recognizing and correcting poor work habits.

Decision Making

- Frequently makes poor decisions.
- Is afraid of risk required to make hard decisions.
- Plays both sides of the fence when making decisions.
- Makes decisions too quickly, thereby regretting decisions made.
- Makes appropriate decisions less often than inappropriate decisions [state approximate percentage of times].
- Makes poor decisions, wasting significant time on the job.
- Needs to weigh options carefully before making decisions.
- Has to take more time in making critical and costly decisions.
- Avoids decision-making opportunities, showing lack of leadership.
- Always requires leadership to back up the decision made.
- Fails to take into account the impact on fellow workers or stakeholders involved.
- Is too analytical; needs to loosen up and go with the gut, at the appropriate time.
- Lacks self-confidence to make tough choices.
- Needs to practice making tougher choices, not just easy-to-please choices.
- Must get more experience in order to use sound judgment in the decision-making process.
- Needs to be exposed to more key decision makers in the organization who can set examples.
- Is too sensitive about hard-core choices that involve large responsibilities.
- Only makes decisions by consensus, even when it is not necessary.
- Should take a decision-making seminar to develop skills.

- Is too comfortable with the status quo, needs to shake things up.
- Cannot commit to a decisive course of action; is too vague.
- Makes too many decisions based on personal feelings, not employee performance.

Empowerment and Delegation

- Has tendency to micromanage.
- Is intimidated by others.
- Is intimidated by younger, more experienced coworkers.
- Will not let go of key projects or pass the baton of succession.
- Lacks delegation skills, which has this person way behind schedule on everything.
- Holds on to the high-profile projects and only delegates small projects.
- Does not show faith in other's capabilities and talents.
- Sends unclear messages about how to get the job done.
- Does not develop staff by giving more responsibility.
- Appears afraid to be "shown up" or "outdone."
- Is intimidated by those more intelligent or more educated.
- Challenges others' credibility by questioning everything they do.
- Never follows up on delegated projects, but criticizes others early on.
- Delegates unfairly, selecting friends first.
- Needs to take a class on delegation.
- Fails to be clear with directions and instructions.
- Hesitates to give power away.
- Is insecure when it comes to empowering others who may be more talented and experienced.
- Makes unnecessary changes in other's work.
- Does not energize the team through delegation.
- Kills synergy with lack of faith in others' ability to do the job.
- Does not challenge workers or raise the bar.
- Encourages status quo behavior.
- Has complacent attitude.

Technical Skill Development

- Allows certification in certain areas to lapse.
- Is not adequately trained to do the job.
- Has inadequate education to do the job.
- Does not possess adequate qualifications and experience to do the job.
- Cannot demonstrate technical skills necessary to do the job well.
- Rarely takes the initiative to update skill base.
- Has encountered difficulty in adapting to technological developments in relevant areas.
- Has not practiced skills in so long that they have eroded.
- Needs refresher course.
- Is a danger to others when operating machinery.
- Inconsistently follows safety and security measures.
- Has been bypassed by new technology.
- Needs to retrain in just one or two areas, but has basic abilities.
- Is not considered a helper by peers.
- Finds problem solving a chore.
- Seems disinterested in the job.
- Has problems in dealing with computerization of equipment.
- Will not take time to review work procedures and new methods of operation.
- Will not willingly anticipate or acquire new skills that will be needed in the future.
- Seems unaware of lack of technical know-how.

People Skills and Relationship Building

- Doesn't seem to really like people.
- Acts like a loner.
- Asks to work alone.
- Does not seem to value relationships.
- Does not build bridges to relationships, but instead destroys them.
- Is demotivational.
- Will not attend company social functions.
- Will not volunteer for any company social functions.
- Does not have the affection and support of staff members.
- Criticizes others frequently.
- Is not helpful.
- Is sarcastic.
- Gives others a hard time.
- Avoids communicating with staff.
- Does not respect issues of confidentiality.
- Embarrasses others.
- Makes jokes at the expense of others' feelings.
- Does not appreciate difference in others and their unique backgrounds or ethnicity.
- Displays prejudiced behavior.
- Does not respect the opposite sex.
- Exhibits borderline sexual harassment behaviors.
- Uses foul language.
- Comments on a person's religion.
- Makes derogatory comments to anyone and everyone.
- Uses intimidation to get what is wanted.
- Spreads stress throughout the work group.
- Talks about others behind their backs.
- Treats others disrespectfully on occasion.

- Is disingenuous.
- Makes people feel nervous or uncomfortable.
- Is manipulative when he or she needs something.
- Is uncomfortable with issues of diversity.
- Has poor interpersonal skills.
- Cannot manage anger well.
- Doesn't listen respectfully to others.
- Has no conflict management skill sets.
- Is not often requested as a work partner.
- Has difficulty relating to others' problems or concerns.
- Is not easily accepted by people from other cultures.
- Does not readily accept people from other cultures.
- Tells inappropriate jokes.
- Is not open to improving relationship skills.
- Offends others easily.
- Is very awkward in social settings.
- Makes little attempt to build rapport.
- Corrects others to embarrass them.
- Tries to feel important by attacking others for no reason.

Coaching Others

- Struggles in facilitating the success of others.
- Dictates rather than delegates.
- Hurts people's feelings.
- Will not coach a successor.
- Is insensitive.
- Does not see coaching as part of the job.
- Struggles to involve people at every level.
- Is not a positive mentor.
- Fails to applaud effort.
- Does not give ongoing encouraging feedback.
- Does not receive feedback in a positive way.
- Is defensive when someone offers a better way.
- Won't give others the chance to discover their own answers.
- Does not inspire others to higher performance.
- Fails to see the potential in others or shine a diamond in the rough.
- Is not easily available or accessible.
- Does not allocate enough time to coach.
- Is a hands-off coach, doesn't get involved easily.
- Is impatient.
- Is very impatient with people who are slow to learn.
- Does not build independence in others.
- Does not see himself or herself as a teacher, guide, and mentor.
- Has difficulty drawing out knowledge and skills in others.
- Gets frustrated with people who make mistakes.
- Will not take time to explain details.
- Assumes others should know how to do something.
- Does not ask probing questions.

Customer Care

- Lacks in understanding the difference between internal and external customer care.
- Does not acknowledge importance of internal customers.
- Cannot relate to customers easily.
- Becomes frustrated or angry with customers.
- Becomes annoyed when a lot of questions are asked by customers.
- Is not always courteous.
- Does not take time to become more knowledgeable for the customer's sake.
- Has poor professional presentation.
- Is arrogant with some difficult customers.
- Does not comprehend the meaning of "recovery and redemption" in relation to customer service.
- Will not practice POS, or Positively Outrageous Service.
- Occasionally argues with customers.
- Clearly does not consider the customer number 1, or even number 2.
- Is not good at problem solving.
- Does not welcome customer complaints well.
- Needs more patience.
- Has to be more resourceful in finding solutions to customer problems.
- Sometimes gets sarcastic or rude with a customer.
- Should take a customer care seminar to sharpen skills.
- Can be condescending at times.
- Ignores customers or fails to acknowledge them when they enter store.
- Often fails to say thank you.
- Forgets to invite the customer back.

- Chews gum or eats candy when talking to customers.
- Is impolite.
- Does not understand that the customer pays the salaries.
- Fails to use common sense when handling customer complaints.
- Does not act empowered to take care of the problem.
- Pushes the problem off on another department.
- Suggests that the customers do business with a competitor if they are not happy.
- Sees the customer as an intruder in the workday instead of a valued partner in business.
- Does not follow up with customers.
- Does not follow up on finding a solution, even after promising to do so.
- Has difficulty in developing a loyal customer base.
- Breaks promises to customers.
- Does not feel very enthusiastic about the company or the products and services offered.
- Lacks pride in work.
- Does not have enthusiasm to serve.
- Wants to wait on upper-level clientele over the average person.
- Demonstrates snobbish attitude at times.
- Loses cool under pressure.
- Is slow moving.
- Provides inaccurate information to client.
- Does not see himself or herself as an extension of the organization.
- Does not view the customer as a partner in business.

Attitude

- Acts aloof.
- Is unapproachable.
- Evidently has low self-esteem.
- Lacks confidence.
- Carries self with poor posture and appears unsure.
- Acts defensively.
- Uses body language in a negative way, for example, rolls eyes, crosses arms, won't make eye contact, sighs loudly, appears irritated or disgusted with matters frequently.
- Approaches people and projects very negatively.
- Sees the glass as half empty, not half full.
- Rarely offers to stay late or help others.
- Takes an "it's not my job" attitude to helping coworkers in need.
- Seems always to have problems.
- Is never cheerful or enthusiastic.
- Is very pessimistic without knowing all the details or people involved.
- Sometimes acts snobbish.
- Has a loser's attitude, "why bother?" approach to everything.
- Is very critical of others, both personally and professionally.
- Rarely cooperates.
- Is rude.
- Lacks manners.
- Views success only in relationship to self and no one else.
- Is not a team player.
- Resents others' successes or accomplishments.
- Quarrels over the slightest matters.
- Feels she or he is never wrong.

- Irritates others with annoying habits.
- Creates tension, or "walking on eggshells" feeling, for the group.
- Never volunteers.
- Is lethargic.
- Takes a "for every silver lining, there is a cloud" attitude when good things happen on the job.
- Projects superior attitude.
- Is a turnoff to fellow employees.
- Never arrives early to a meeting or to work.
- Lacks "can-do" belief system.

Handling Personal Problems

- Struggles to balance work and home life.
- Is late often for meetings and work.
- Complains frequently about home life.
- Does not seem to have adequate support system at home.
- Appears depressed.
- Has used alcohol and pills while on the job.
- Will not take advantage of employee counseling at work.
- Will not pursue help from EAP (Employee Assistance Program), or other valuable resources available within the company.
- Talks excessively to others about personal problems.
- Always seems to have a problem going on.
- Often has personal problems that interfere with productivity.
- Has family that makes constant interruptions in the workday.
- Seems stressed out.
- Appears to be tired a lot.
- Is often distracted from the task at hand.
- Does not understand the link between personal problems and work-related problems.
- Complains about financial worries.
- Cannot get organized.
- Worries about children or other family members all day at work.
- Appears to have inadequate child care arrangements, which causes stress.
- Refuses to seek counseling.
- Denies having personal difficulties.
- Has unresolved performance issues from working in another department.

- Cannot seem to manage stress.
- Loses temper easily.
- Exhibits low self-esteem.
- Seems in denial about the facts.
- Is more comfortable in the victim role.
- Has little or no outside interests of any kind.
- Has come to work bruised or badly shaken emotionally.
- Has personal problems that have drastically impacted overall performance.
- Will not admit to being depressed often.

Creativity and Innovation

- Cannot think outside the box.
- Will not consider blowing up the box.
- Is too uptight, needs to let down guard.
- Does not know how to effectively brainstorm, instead "brain drizzles."
- Rarely, if ever, has new ideas.
- Doesn't seem to understand how innovation moves a career forward.
- Never offers a new idea.
- Seems to lack the level of creativity required to excel.
- Copies others' ideas.
- Is never original.
- Integrates what others have already done successfully.
- Has ideas lacking in pizzazz.
- Never wants to be part of the creative process.
- Appears intimidated by others' ideas.
- Tries to jump on the bandwagon of someone else's ideas and innovative thinking.
- Cannot see what is right in front of him or her.
- Has not demonstrated any visioning skills so far.
- Cannot come up with one innovative idea for client.
- Never experiments with new approaches.
- Cannot accept colors, fashions, trends, or styles outside the norm.
- Never wows people with a great new concept.
- Always prefers the tried and true over new and innovative.
- Is never radical.
- Does not contribute new ideas that save the company money.
- Does not come up with ways to get new clients.

- Cannot see things from a unique angle.
- Lacks imaginative vision.
- Has no flair for the latest ideas on the market.
- Rarely solves problems with a unique perspective.
- Has a rusty imagination process.
- Only colors inside the lines, so to speak.

Meeting Deadlines

- Unable to estimate the time it takes to get the job done.
- Will not tell anyone when a delay is anticipated.
- Takes on too many projects at once.
- Waits to the last minute to get the job done.
- Is always behind schedule, never ahead.
- Cannot stay on task.
- Is easily distracted by something more interesting.
- Cannot effectively block out distractions.
- Misses most deadlines.
- Cannot seem to understand reasons for missing deadlines.
- Repeats deadline-missing behaviors over and over.
- Requires way too much supervision to meet a deadline.
- Finds pressure deadlines to be extremely difficult.
- Will take all the time needed to meet a deadline, even if there is ample time and more available.
- Cannot seem to manage time well when it comes to deadline pressures.
- Not suited to short-deadline work projects.
- Will not admit to missing a deadline.
- Makes excuses for missing a deadline.
- Gets flustered easily as a deadline approaches.
- Needs to better understand performance goals and the impact on others.
- Cannot connect the direct link between missed deadlines and other functions within the company.
- Struggles with staying focused on what's most important.
- Has difficulty prioritizing.
- Is too dependent on others.

Leadership Skills

- Has difficulty motivating others.
- Does not contribute to a high-morale environment.
- Is reluctant to share blame or take blame.
- Doesn't walk the talk or set the example.
- Does not garner loyalty from others.
- Has difficulty earning respect.
- Has difficulty trusting and being trusted.
- Does not support training, personal, or professional development.
- Will not make effort to sharpen skills on own time.
- Wants to be liked more than lead.
- Is afraid to champion a movement.
- Won't share successes.
- Has difficulty setting goals and action plans.
- Has a hard time focusing.
- Is easily distracted and nonattentive.
- Lacks humility.
- Needs to sharpen leadership traits, such as integrity, communication skills, and trust.
- Wants to talk more than listen.
- Treats people rudely.
- Does not put people first.
- Cannot see the whole person, just the worker.
- Lacks confident demeanor.
- Sets unrealistic goals.
- Does not involve others in leadership decisions.
- Will not easily solicit others' opinions.
- Has not yet demonstrated strong leadership character.
- Prefers to dictate rather than lead.

- Puts high productivity ahead of safety and employee welfare.
- Seems to lack understanding and has not demonstrated the company's core values.
- Sometimes acts in contradiction to the organization's mission and vision.
- Cannot convey a personal leadership vision.
- Holds back on relaying vital leadership information.
- Is a developing leader, but not strong yet in many areas that require tough action and decision making.
- Appears insecure about taking the lead when asked to do so.
- Avoids disputes.
- Does not perform well in meetings.
- Has difficulty being punctual.
- Has not yet gained the respect of others.
- Misfiles or frequently loses paperwork.
- Is not adept at managing new hires.
- Has been the subject of more than two grievances in 12 months.
- Does not understand the concept of project management or planning.
- Has poor hiring and firing skills.
- Does not understand concepts of strategic planning.
- Has no succession plan in place.
- Exhibits intrusive behavior.
- Makes poor use of time.
- Does not facilitate the success of others willingly.
- Would not be found guilty of integrity, if it were a crime.

Negotiation Skills

- Takes a win-lose approach over a win-win approach.
- Has an "I'm going down and I'm taking you with me" attitude to mistakes.
- Lacks attention to the needs of other stakeholders.
- Forgets to consider contingencies.
- Doesn't ask key questions for the benefit of both parties.
- Has negotiations that often result in a negative attitude toward the organization.
- Has agreements that often end in lose-lose, rather than win-win.
- Does not prepare sufficiently for negotiations ahead of time.
- Tries to take advantage of others.
- Gets too emotional; loses control of temper.
- Forgets to get the legal department to sign off on contracts.
- Has clients that usually come away not happy with agreements made.
- Drives a wedge between the organization and the customer.
- Has fewer and fewer negotiations that go smoothly anymore.
- Does not voluntarily inform leadership of progress on negotiations.
- Will not take accountability for failed negotiations.
- Will not ask for legal advice when it is called for during negotiations.
- Never takes others' opinions or viewpoints into account.
- Needs improvement on understanding the give and take of negotiations.

- Lacks finesse with clients.
- Puts self first over company's interests or reputation.
- Is in it for the kill, or the commission, not the long-term relationship with the organization and its people.
- Needs to use less emotional behavior and more reason in negotiations.
- Should consider a seminar to sharpen skills in this area.
- Fails to seek out additional options.

Appearance

- Chews gum on the job and in front of customers.
- Is a sloppy dresser.
- Has a hygiene problem.
- Does not clean and press uniform.
- Does not comb hair.
- Has unclean fingernails.
- Has worn, unpolished shoes.
- Has dirty and wrinkled clothes.
- Wears excessive makeup.
- Smells of cigarette smoke.
- Has body odor, resulting in complaints from coworkers.
- Appears unprofessional.
- Fails to take pride in appearance.
- Does not see appearance related to how the company appears as well.
- Does not groom facial hair.
- Ignores requests to improve appearance.
- Has mismatched pieces of clothing.
- Does not carry self with confidence.
- Is always disheveled.
- Underdresses for professional meetings.
- Projects a negative image of the company.
- Is uninviting; people request to be seated away from this person.
- Has an unpolished look.
- Eats with mouth open.
- Is lacking in manners and appropriate social conduct.

Self-Esteem and Confidence

- Acts shy, not confident.
- Will not speak up in a meeting.
- Is easily intimidated.
- Walks with poor posture.
- Will not make eye contact.
- Always puts himself or herself down.
- Is very negative toward personal accomplishments.
- Does not accept compliments well.
- Lacks ability to stand up for self.
- Shrugs off praise of any kind.
- Appears angry with self.
- Exhibits defensive behavior.
- Has a bad attitude.
- Presents a low self-image.
- Acts unworthy.
- Never wants to be in company photographs.
- Uses negative self-talk phrases, such as "I hate the way I look" or "I am so stupid."
- Is always the victim.
- Has an appearance that reflects low self-esteem.
- Shies away from taking risks or looking foolish.
- Never puts himself or herself in a position to be the focus of attention.
- Will not admit to low self-esteem getting in the way of higher performance and productivity.

Efficient Use of Time

- Wastes time.
- Does not handle time crunches well.
- Cannot prioritize.
- Gets off track easily.
- Spends too much time socializing.
- Daydreams frequently.
- Cannot handle emergencies when they arise.
- Needs a strict schedule to accomplish anything.
- Is not flexible.
- Does not deliver work in the time frame promised.
- Does not manage interruptions well.
- Does not set boundaries for intrusions.
- Needs to use a daily planner or Palm Pilot.
- Needs to get organized.
- Is very disorganized.
- Procrastinates a lot.
- Overextends self.
- Will not delegate.
- Will not ask for help.
- Needs to break down projects into doable parts.
- Has difficulty working smarter, rather than harder and longer.
- Makes too many personal calls.
- Has too many personal visitors.

Problem Solving and Conflict Resolution

- Has insufficient problem-solving skills.
- Is weak at analyses of problems.
- Does not completely analyze the whole picture.
- Does not seek help from others.
- Cannot easily track patterns of behavior in recurring problems.
- Uses poor judgment in solving most problems.
- Uses one-size-fits-all approach to problem solving.
- Ignores systemic problems in the organization.
- Does not anticipate likely problems before they happen.
- Is not strong at developing alternative solutions.
- Uses emotion, not logic, in analyzing evidence and facts.
- Will not offer solutions for fear of being wrong.
- Looks to others to find and fix problems.
- Never goes beneath the surface of the issue at hand.
- Has weak analysis skills.
- Needs to attend a problem-solving training program.
- Lacks confidence to recommend timely solutions.
- Waits too long to try and solve a problem.
- Tends to make conflicts worse, not better.
- Avoids confrontation at all costs.
- Avoids escalation.
- Fails to look for common ground.
- Makes enemies out of friends.
- Does not compromise; the concept escapes all thinking.
- Gets defensive and frustrated.
- Often needs to have leadership step in to resolve a conflict.
- Is too stubborn.
- Has an attitude that contributes to conflict.
- Has low self-worth that contributes to conflict.

- Does not use diplomacy.
- Forgets to look for the common ground.
- Does not appreciate and respect the differences in others.
- Cannot act as a third party in handling disputes; looks for a fourth party to get involved.
- Rarely gives in, even when wrong.
- Allows trivial matters to rule the situation.
- Resorts to blaming others.
- Gets to a point where yielding for the good of others is out of the question.
- Is a poor listener.
- Gets way too emotional.
- Attacks the person personally.
- Cannot keep things on a professional level.
- Allows stress to rule in lieu of resolution.
- Cannot see conflict solutions available in most cases, large and small.
- Does not build loyalty from the ranks.
- Needs to attend a conflict resolution training program.
- Will not look beyond obvious options.

Teamwork

- Rarely gets consensus before moving forward on something.
- Cannot operate without consensus.
- Has great difficulty leading teams.
- Never demonstrates teamwork in action.
- Seems to lack necessary skills to participate in team action.
- Cannot work within or between teams effectively.
- Resents being part of a group.
- Looks for all the glory.
- Does not want to share recognition or achievement.
- Holds back information pertinent to the team's success.
- Has difficulty in getting along with others.
- Is arrogant in nature.
- Gets frustrated by depending on others.
- Is mostly a pessimistic team player.
- Will not commit to team goals and objectives.
- Is motivated by his or her own aims and objectives rather than the team itself.
- Is not perceived as a team player by other team members or leaders.
- Fails to coordinate projects with others.
- Keeps getting reassigned to different teams before the project concludes.
- Has been removed from numerous teams for inability to cooperate or for holding back the process
- Slacks off and lets others do the work.
- Has no team spirit.
- Lacks pride in the project and the team.

Emotional Intelligence

- Assumes that a college degree gives him or her the right to be promoted ahead of others who may be more qualified.
- Does not understand that emotional intelligence, or EQ, is a stronger attribute than IQ.
- Thinks IQ is the only measure of success.
- Will not use emotional intelligence competencies to write job descriptions.
- Will not consider using emotional intelligence competencies for matching employees to the right training.
- Does not consider emotional intelligence competencies when hiring new people.
- Focuses too much on résumés with higher education qualities than skills necessary to do the job.
- Has high IQ but cannot get along with others.
- Is a smart worker, but lacks common sense.
- Does not accept that there are wide varieties of intelligences that contribute to the organization's success.
- Needs to read *Emotional Intelligence: Why It Can Matter More than IQ* and *Working with Emotional Intelligence*, both authored by Daniel Goleman.
- Uses education as a tool of entitlement.
- Has an aggressive personality; is difficult to work with.
- Has intelligence that allows him or her to argue well and leave others feeling hurt.
- Uses IQ to put others down.
- Uses IQ against those who do not have the benefit of higher education.

- Does not fully recognize the importance of soft-skill intelligence.
- Cannot list soft-skill intelligences required to do the job well.

Overall Productivity

- Has lower productivity than he or she should, given background and skill sets.
- Takes too much time to get the job completed.
- Wastes time.
- Does not seem to care about her or his own performance level.
- Drags the team down with poor performance.
- Paces slowly on all projects.
- Appears bored frequently.
- Does not appear underchallenged.
- Seems fatigued.
- Is physically unfit to handle job requirements.
- Is clumsy.
- Is prone to accidents.
- Does not seem mentally or physically ready to do the job required.
- Is not motivated.
- Has low morale.
- Is always asking, "What is in it for me?" before offering to serve others.
- Has low job accuracy.
- Needs to improve productivity by [provide percentage] by [provide date].
- Misses productions goals frequently.
- Despite coaching and training, productivity remains low.
- Produces work that must always be checked by others.
- Is one of the lowest producers in the department.
- Is careless and makes lots of mistakes.
- Seems to understand standards required, but cannot produce within them.

- Lets personal problems interfere with job performance.
- Has low product knowledge.
- Will not take initiative to learn about new products.
- Has a superficial understanding of processes.
- Never troubleshoots.

Loyalty

- Talks behind people's backs.
- Does not respect confidentiality.
- Sides with competitors first.
- Shows no loyalty to the organization, even after several years.
- Feels entitled.
- Does not take pride in his or her job and the overall operations of the organization.
- Is disrespectful to leadership.
- Talks negatively about leadership.
- Talks negatively about the company.
- Behaves inappropriately outside of the company; does not see that he or she is a representative of the organization's culture and reputation.
- Fights being a part of the culture.
- Is not trusted by fellow workers.
- Acts very suspicious of everyone, almost paranoid.
- Won't give anyone the benefit of the doubt.
- Has a defensive attitude.
- Does not display an "all for one, one for all" attitude.
- Does not like being part of a team effort.
- Looks for ways to embarrass others or the organization.
- Is not a dedicated person.
- Is not devoted to anyone or anything.
- Will not stand up for anyone.
- Is a very conditional friend and coworker; unconditional support not an option.

Resistance to Change

- Equates any change with loss.
- Resists all types of change, thereby holding back progress of the team.
- Is suspicious of all change.
- Does not adapt easily.
- Fears change.
- Will not take risks.
- Lacks confidence when change arises.
- Has a difficult time getting on board with new processes.
- Does not welcome new and better ways of doing things.
- Seems intimidated that change will outdate him or her.
- Never initiates change.
- Has a hard time embracing change of any kind.
- Cannot adapt to the speed at which change takes place in the work world.
- Is intimidated and hesitant to learn anything computerized.
- Will not take computer classes.
- Cannot comprehend a global work environment.
- Does not welcome diversity.
- Insists on doing things the old way, even when there is a faster, better way to do it.
- Argues with people about making changes.
- Holds on to old habits.
- Does not welcome working with younger, new team members.
- Cannot appreciate new opportunities that may result from change.
- Is forced into change.
- Will follow the group to change only if forced to.

- Does not demonstrate skills or effort to anticipate upcoming changes.
- Fights management every step of the way when change is presented.

Project Management

- Seems to miss the various aspects of project management.
- Is always over budget.
- Often misses time frames and deadlines.
- Does not select the most qualified people for the team.
- Does not keep teammates.
- Does not fully understand how to use project-planning tools.
- Wastes resources and time.
- Has poor planning skills.
- Is not a rainmaker, doesn't bring new projects in to the organization.
- Does not interact well with other project members.
- Is poor at coordinating resources to bring the project to fruition.
- Relays information poorly, resulting in poor project communications.
- Cannot seem to bring a project to an effective closure or desired result.
- Does not come up with his or her own system for keeping the project on track.
- Repeatedly has problems that stall the project.
- Is not familiar with product lines.
- Doesn't weigh cost/benefit ratios.
- Is not an effective multitasker.
- Fails to remember essential tasks.
- Cannot coordinate two projects simultaneously.
- Cannot maintain project management log.
- Does not use project management software effectively.
- Misses milestones on every project.
- Misses details.

- Raises stress level as complexity increases on the job.
- Rarely considers cost-effective options.
- Could exercise greater control.
- Is seen as hoarding power.
- Does not make decisions in a timely manner.
- Chooses people to work with who may not be best suited for the project.
- Doesn't take time to carefully review competencies of all project members.
- Tries to be popular rather than a leader.

Safety

- Violates safety regulations.
- Ignores safety rules and guidelines.
- Does not always wear safety gear.
- "Looks the other way" when someone else abuses safety rules.
- Does not value safe working procedures.
- Has a safety record that could be better.
- Has a poor safety record.
- Does not maintain all equipment to safety standards.
- Does not encourage safety practices among workers.
- Could be stricter when enforcing safety.
- Puts productivity ahead of safety.
- Ignores no-smoking signs.
- Has on occasion been a danger to others.
- Uses safety equipment only when told to do so.
- Has allowed the team to suffer several avoidable accidents under his or her supervision.
- Is complacent.
- Gets distracted when full focus is required on the job, for safety reasons.
- Tolerates hazardous conditions.
- Makes excuses when safety is jeopardized.
- Does not take safety seriously enough.
- Could use a refresher course on safety issues.
- Has a lax attitude toward safety.
- Is not instinctive about safety.
- Has had too many incidents occur under her or his watch.

Goal Setting

- Displays little or no interest in setting goals.
- Pays little or no attention to aims and objectives.
- Does not set goals high enough.
- Has goals that are too lofty and impractical.
- Does not link goal setting to long-term success.
- Is not easily guided by goals and objectives.
- Hesitates to work with leadership to set appropriate goals.
- Does not use vision to see the big picture.
- Questions expectations for higher job performance.
- Is not self-directed.
- Is not an initiator.
- Sets vague goals.
- Blames others for not achieving goals.
- Needs to work on achieving several goals at one time.
- Is uncomfortable being held accountable for achievement.
- Is unreliable.
- Finds that tough situations are too much for him or her to handle.
- Denies failure.
- Has basic goals that seem unreachable.
- Needs to learn how to map out a plan to reach goals.
- Needs someone to guide the process the first time goals are planned.
- Needs to learn how to alter goals when necessary.
- Has difficulty phrasing objectives.
- Cannot decide what path to take to reach the desired end result.
- Lacks self-confidence, which appears to be interfering with achievement.
- Lets everyday problems deflect from goals.

- Rarely offers to help anyone else achieve their goals.
- Cannot juggle more than one thing at a time.
- Makes excuses for everything.
- Uses poor judgment to meet deadlines.
- Often lets down team members when a specific objective has to be met.
- Cannot see the big picture when the rest of the team can.
- Gets overwhelmed if there are too many details.
- Is easily bored.
- Allows too many details to fall through the cracks.
- Has a short attention span.
- Never documents details of a project so that others can track progress.
- Thinks that progress is keeping busy, not necessarily accomplishing the goal.
- Does not manage money well.
- Lobbies for more help than is needed to get the job done.
- Needs to read books or get training on setting and achieving goals.

Motivation and Morale Building

- Motivation is extrinsic rather than intrinsic.
- Has a negative influence on others.
- Uses fear as a motivator.
- Uses intimidation as a motivator.
- Does not believe in personal growth motivation.
- Will not recognize that retention is an extension of keeping people's morale high.
- Wonders why turnover is so high.
- Purposely puts the kibosh on positive attitudes.
- Cannot sustain high morale and positive motivation.
- Turns a positive workplace into a negative workplace and has poor attitude.
- Has low self-esteem.
- Has an angry personality.
- Communicates poorly.
- Sees the company as more of a corporation, not a community of workers.
- Does not respect the "whole person."
- Does not factor fun into the workplace.
- Is incapable of unleashing employee synergy.
- Is not respected.
- Is not considered a good influence.
- Does not prepare teams for success and fun.
- Cannot understand basic human emotional needs.
- Is too control-oriented.
- Rarely assumes the best in others.
- Rarely gives the benefit of the doubt.
- Is a Theory X worker.
- Always wants to know what is in it for him or her.
- Does not encourage teamwork.

- Celebrates seldom.
- Stays in the office.
- Does not enjoy rewarding performance or celebrating successes.
- Does not inspire vision.
- Gives phony flattery, not real praise and recognition.
- Does not readily show compassion or caring for others.
- Takes no part in esprit de corps.

Common Sense and Good Judgment

- Does not plan for contingencies.
- Fails to use common sense.
- Has poor judgment.
- Has no foresight.
- Cannot make good decisions off the cuff.
- Plans to ask for forgiveness, not permission.
- Is always rushed.
- Does not stop to think first, then speak.
- Makes simple situations more complicated than they are.
- Takes the more difficult route to solution finding.
- Dramatizes everything out of proportion.
- Fears that if something is simple, it will not appear smart.
- Has skewed logic.
- Does not see the obvious.
- Gets too many people involved in simple issues.
- Makes easy-to-fix problems greater than they are.
- Behaves in a way that is demotivating to other employees.
- Will not take advice that makes more sense in the long run.
- Wants others to take the responsibility.
- Will not stick her or his neck out.

Personal Growth and Development

- Does not aspire to reach higher potential.
- Takes a lazy approach to most things.
- Always uses the path of least resistance and risk.
- Does not read books.
- Does not read newspapers or magazines.
- Appears unaware of world events, politics, or general news.
- Stops trying early on.
- Follows the crowd.
- Always wants to watch TV on breaks.
- Doesn't display any individual style or spunk.
- Has no plan for future development and growth.
- Doesn't care that GED is the only educational credential he or she has.
- Has a one-track mind.
- Assumes that everyone else is going to win, so why bother trying.
- Assumes victim role in most situations.
- Consumed with self-pity.
- Difficulty balancing work and family.
- Has few outside interests.
- Has unresolved alcohol and drug problems.
- Behaves as if he or she is in denial.
- Refuses help when it's offered.
- Lets personal issues negatively impact work.
- Is overly sensitive to feedback of any kind.
- Shuts down and won't communicate.
- Is immature.

Professional Growth and Intentional Learning

- Rarely seeks out ways to grow skill sets.
- Never asks to attend seminars or training functions.
- Sees job as a dead end.
- Does not investigate higher-education learning opportunities, even if the company is willing to pay for it.
- Does not take initiative on the job.
- Shows initiative far below capabilities.
- Seems lazy.
- Doesn't display intentional learning of new skills and ideas.
- Waits until directed to take action.
- Has very little independent action.
- Does not read books.
- Does not read trade magazines or journals.
- Is unaware of latest goings on in the industry.
- Will not take advantage of career counseling when offered.
- Will not apply for a higher-level, higher-paying position.
- Shies away from taking risks with his or her present job status.
- Stops trying early on.
- Has personal issues that negatively impact work, especially in regards to promotions.
- Cuts corners.
- Sacrifices authenticity for productivity.
- Is sometimes unethical.
- Makes frequent judgment errors.
- Misses the mark on representing the professional standards for the job.
- Does not keep commitments.

- Occasionally lies.
- Does not dress to professional standards.
- Lacks professional ethics.
- Lacks business etiquette.

Part Two

Lessons from the Best

World-Class Organizations: Their Perfect Phrases, Strategies, and Unique Approaches to Preventing Employee Performance Problems

You've heard of practicing preventative medicine. Well there's preventative medicine in the business world too, but it's a different kind of prevention. You don't have to swallow pills or run on the treadmill 20 minutes every day to achieve it. You do, however, have to take a healthier approach to preventing employee problems whenever possible. That approach might be in the form of a phrase, a slogan, a special technique, or a strategy—straightforward measures that quickly get to the heart of matters.

The ideas and practices in this section of the book come from world-class organizations and their leaders—all noticeably effective in their leadership styles. All have proven track records when it comes to creating high-performing workplaces and conducting business in a way that actually helps prevent employee performance problems from growing. A platform is thereby created for peak performers to launch ahead and sometimes even celebrate, or accept and discuss openly, their mistakes.

When it comes to perfect phrases and the strategies that really breathe life into the workplace, there are lots of organizations that are doing it right. Here you'll find not only their phrases, but also their philosophies and one-of-a-kind approaches to making it happen—bite-size chunks of wisdom from the best in the business.

Here are some of them.

General Electric

GE is a company rich in history. Founded by Thomas Edison more than a century ago, former CEO Jack Welch inherited one of the world's most sacred institutions and practiced some of the following perfect phrases to avoid performance problems while creating unprecedented, off-the-charts performance ratings during his reign:

- Don't be afraid to buck conventional wisdom.
- Avoid the minutiae.
- Don't think that you or your company has all the answers.
- Numbers aren't the vision. Numbers are the product.
- Never bully or intimidate.
- Don't punish yourself—or anyone else—for falling short of a stretch goal.

Saturn

It's no secret that most people do not enjoy car shopping. To overcome this adversity, the people at Saturn car company have taken a new approach, using a simple philosophy and slogan. The company's slogan is a perfect phrase that speaks for itself:

People First.

In the automobile business this can be something of an anomaly.

JetBlue

JetBlue continues its quest to provide low-fare, hassle-free, high-quality airline service. A few of the perfect phrases used by the airline for measuring ongoing performance and avoiding pitfalls include the following from JetBlue's two-way, employee/employer commitment:

JetBlue's Commitment and Accountability Phrases to Its Employees

- We always will have open, honest, and two-way communication.
- We will provide you with a work environment free from all forms of harassment.
- You will have the opportunity to express your career aspirations and have them acted upon.
- We will return your business-related phone calls within 24 hours.
- We will provide you with the orientation training and proper tools to be successful in your job.

Employees' Commitment and Accountability Phrases to JetBlue

- I will support and use JetBlue-sponsored training and education programs.
- I will treat individual customers for who they truly are: They are the reason we exist!
- I take care of and protect JetBlue assets.
- I am completely honest in my communication with JetBlue employees.
- I take personal responsibility for my decisions, actions, and professional growth.
- Other performance metrics include a monthly report to everyone in the company detailing 10 performance issues, such as how the airline is doing in terms of lost baggage, on-time performance, and flight completion.

eBay

eBay continues to build a worldwide culture of trust and high performance and uses these five basic principles of operation as their strategy:

- We believe people are basically good.
- We believe everyone has something to contribute.
- We believe that an honest, open environment can bring out the best in people.
- We recognize and respect everyone as a unique individual.
- We encourage you to treat others the way you want to be treated.

London Business School

In order to measure the success and ongoing performance levels of their students, the prestigious business school developed what is called a Transformational-Benchmarking Questionnaire. The tool surveys graduates using the following questions as perfect phrases for gathering critical performance data:

- How much of the program that you took do you recall?
- Do you stay in touch with faculty?
- How big an impact has the program had on your career and on your quality of life?

Survey results provide detailed information about the performance of each student. Leaders then evaluate that performance against the school's goal of creating a transformational experience for every London Business School student.

Amazon.com

Jeff Bezos continues to change the economics of the book industry with his vision for becoming a cyber-bookstore with the world's largest selection. But all of this takes top performance and avoidance of performance pitfalls. Here are a few Amazonian strategies and phrases:

- Have clarity about your purpose. Top management must be able to answer the question, "Why are we here?"
- Know where you are going. Long-term strategies should come from the top.
- Ask where you are now. What are the strengths, weaknesses, opportunities, and challenges?
- Practice using a strategic planning triage. Identify short-term goals for the business consistent with the purpose and vision of the company.
- Develop strategies for each outcome. Strategies are broader efforts for achieving each of the core outcomes.
- Develop tactics. Step-by-step actions will be taken to achieve each strategy.

American Express

If you're going to try to prevent performance problems and create a workplace of cooperation, you need esprit de corps, or team spirit. At American Express this is done successfully and touted in their well-known slogan of human performance and customer acceptance—*Membership has its privileges*. It's no secret that when performance is the issue, group identity is key in this highly respected financial institution. The slogan would also imply that when esprit de corps is missing, productivity and success could suffer.

IKEA

The hip and innovative Swedish furniture company IKEA banks on employee admiration and respect by keeping their global philosophies consistent and building pride within the organization—no matter what languages you speak. IKEA stakes its high performance and achievement on internal pride and enthusiasm using such methods as:

- A code of ethics for its suppliers worldwide
- Standing up for global child-labor protection laws
- Seeking education for women and children in remote third-world countries

Gallup

According to this highly reputable polling company, the greatest source of satisfaction and production on the job is rooted in both emotional and personal needs. Gallup's take on employee performance isn't about money or benefits, but rather *the quality of the relationship between employees and their supervisors.*

Target

A performance-driven risk taker who works at Target, one of the nation's top retailers, with more than 280,000 employees and locations in 47 states, might well use the following Target phrases to describe himself or herself.

- Loves fun and challenging work
- Appreciates feedback because it contributes to professional development and growth
- Wants to be part of a socially responsible organization that gives more than $2 million a week to the communities it serves
- A person with a great sense of individuality
- Someone who recognizes the importance of diversity

A few Target corporate phrases include *Whatever the experience, you are Target Corporation* and *You are excited and you should be.*

The Ritz-Carlton Hotels

Ritz-Carlton General Manager Myra deGersdorff explains how her award-winning organization takes strategy and performance to a higher level and how its 20 Gold Standards of performance and customer service pave the way:

> During every shift, in every department, at 35 Ritz-Carlton properties around the world, 17,000 employees start their day by discussing the importance of one of the 20 Gold Standards practiced by the company. On that exact same day, every employee at The Ritz-Carlton hotels around the world is discussing the same Gold Standard. When employees reach the 20th Gold Standard, which by the way all employees carry with them on the job as a small folded card, they start over again.

A few of the Gold Standard phrases include:

- To create pride and joy in the workplace, all employees have the right to be involved in the planning of the work that affects them.
- Each employee is empowered. For example, when a guest has a problem or needs something special, you should break away from your regular duties to address and resolve the issue.
- Take pride in and care of your personal appearance. Everyone is responsible for conveying a professional image by adhering to Ritz-Carlton clothing and grooming standards.

Can you imagine the synchronicity an organization gains when all of its people are following and believing in the same goals and objectives, at the same time, whether that be in London or in San Francisco? The Ritz-Carlton's efforts have paid off more than once, as winner of the prestigious Malcolm

Baldrige National Quality Award—the first and only hotel company ever to receive such an honor.

Whole Foods

Whole Foods is all teams when it comes to performance. It's also the largest natural foods grocery chain in the United States. Here are a few of their mantras and practices for removing misinformed conjecture and rumors that may hinder performance and productivity:

- All for one and one for all!
- Every team member at every level shall have access to the organization's operating and financial data.
- CEO's compensation is capped at 10 times the average team member's pay.
- Previous year's salaries and bonuses are posted by name for every employee.
- Only teams have the power to approve candidates for full-time employment and it takes a two-thirds majority vote from the team to hire someone.

Hewlett-Packard

Carly Fiorina was Hewlett-Packard's first female chairman and chief executive officer. HP is a leading global provider of computing and imaging solutions and services. The following is a phrase attributed to Ms. Fiorina in regard to people performance.

> Leadership is performance. You have to be conscious about your behavior, because everyone else is.

Nordstrom

The two most notable phrases from the highly popular retailer Nordstrom contain the following two rules:

1. Use your good judgment in all situations.
2. There will be no other rules.

Virgin Group

Known for its wildly famous Gonzo Branding and fabulous performance of its people, the Virgin Group comprises 350 companies and remains a most unusual conglomerate of success and peak production. Although most of its revenues come from airlines, megastores, and mobile phones, the rest comes from hundreds of small ventures like Virgin cosmetics and Virgin Wines.

On March 30, 2000, Richard Branson, entrepreneur and founder of the Virgin Group, became Sir Richard Branson, knighted for his services to entrepreneurship in a ceremony at Buckingham Palace. With typical élan, Branson is known for articulating several phrases when it comes to achieving peak performance in one of his companies:

- Don't lead sheep, herd cats.
- Streamline decision making.
- Act as a catalyst.
- Encourage chaos.
- Make good ideas welcome (wherever they come from).
- Blur the divide between work and play.
- Never say never.
- Nice guys finish first.

Intel

At Intel, values are at the heart of this amazing company's production and people performance. In addition, Intel is an organization dedicated to improving the lives of its employees worldwide, both in and out of the office. When it comes to performance, Intel implements many of the following phrases and more:

- Assume responsibility.
- Execute flawlessly.
- Constructively confront and solve problems.
- Work as a team with respect and trust for one another.
- Be open and direct.
- Listen to all ideas and viewpoints.
- Do the right things right.
- Take pride in our work.
- Foster innovation and creative thinking.
- Embrace change and challenge the status quo.
- Ensure a safe, clean, and injury-free workplace.
- Make it easy to work with us.

Whether it's customer service, discipline, risk-taking, or executing ideas, Intel has lots of perfect phrases, including this one by Intel cofounder Robert Noyce: "Do not be encumbered by history. Go off and do something wonderful."

Microsoft

It is said that Bill Gates and Microsoft continue to dominate the high ground of the Information Superhighway. You might think that such a high-tech organization might be low touch when it comes to coaching employees for greater performance—not so. Here are some of the phrases used by Microsoft when it comes to facilitating the success of their people in an amazingly fast-moving and enormously competitive industry.

- Challenge people's weaknesses by giving them new responsibilities.

- Give employees opportunities that expose them to upper-level management.
- Walk a mile in someone else's shoes. Let employees spend a day in another department to see what goes on and observe performance.
- Lead by example.

DHL

DHL takes a high-level view when it comes to tackling performance issues worldwide and, thereby, focuses on the importance of corporate citizenship in the world's highly competitive global delivery and shipping industry. Performance phrases attributed to the ever-growing global logistics provider include the following:

- DHL believes it is as important to be a corporate citizen of the world as much as it is to be a corporation.
- For DHL, responding quickly to customers' needs and working in partnership with them to provide solutions to their commercial needs is key.
- DHL contends that good corporate citizenship is a fundamental part of achieving sustained value creation for both society and the company.
- All DHL employees are encouraged to take local action in support of causes about which they feel strongly.
- Working here is not about a job. It's about a passion, a drive to deliver, striving to be the best in all we do.
- When it comes to global performance, DHL's team of more than 170,000 dedicated employees is committed to making DHL the U.S. and international industry leader.

Get the Big Picture on Performance

In the first part of this book, we started out by examining the depth of dozens of employee performance problems and how to document them clearly and with meaning. In this second section, we have focused on the greater breadth of employee performance—not only as it relates to documenting employee performance problems, but also as it relates to employee performance in general. Each example acknowledges the wide variety of perfect phrases, strategies, and unique approaches to performance issues being used today by world-class organizations all over the globe.

Being able to reference these practical, here-and-now techniques is what broadens a manager's scope with regards to evaluating performance matters in the real world. It's a tool for getting the big picture and stepping outside the performance box. When we take time to look at other organizations' management and leadership styles and learn from them, we gain deeper perspective and insight that can carry us forward through our most difficult employee decisions, problems, and hurdles. We may not all share the same industry concerns, but universally, as managers, we share very similar people performance and productivity issues.

It is in this section that a manager can learn a bit more about adaptability and appreciation for others' leadership talents and performance situations. We can all relate to these situations, regardless of where we live, how we do our jobs, or why we select the performance standards of excellence that we choose to implement.

Part Three

Additional Tips and Techniques

Part Three

Fast and Easy Ways for Measuring Improvement Resulting from Well-Documented Performance Issues

---

Perfect Phrases for Documenting Team Performance Problems

- [Team member names go here] appear to be sabotaging the overall efforts of the team by [give examples, for example, missing deadlines or withholding information].
- This team is having a difficult time acting in a self-directed manner and needs more hand holding than the other teams do.
- Levels of performance, given the caliber of the team members, are lower than they should be.
- Members of this team are not sharing information willingly.
- Senior members of the team are not relaying their expectations, or vision for the organization, clearly so that others can take appropriate action.
- Not all team members are aware of new policies that affect the group.
- This team is having a difficult time with various cross-functional aspects of performance, and they seem to concentrate only on one area repeatedly.

- Execution of ideas is being hindered by certain teammates.
- Delivery of new product ideas and services is not as seamless as it should be.
- The psychological aspects of distance appear to be stopping this group from becoming a fine-tuned, high-performing virtual team.
- There seems to be key talent missing from this team.
- Conflict is apparent among these team members.
- The team lacks the team spirit necessary to motivate others involved.
- Team members hesitate to take the ball and run with it.
- This team doesn't seem to understand the important issues at stake, nor do they seem to take this project seriously.
- Teammates are not communicating effectively and frequently enough for success.
- There appears to be a lack of confidence among team members.
- The team is being dominated by one or two key players and the rest are not getting a chance to contribute equally.
- Performance difficulties continue to surface with this particular group.

Here in the third section of this book, you'll start with a few fast and easy-to-use tools that can help you to quickly measure the performances you've been documenting up to this point. It's important for managers to learn a wide variety of measurement techniques, and the easier and quicker they are to implement, the better. Effective, yet easy-to-implement measurement tools not only help a manager to gauge what's getting accomplished but they also help to develop employees' ongoing success and confidence. These tools also help to determine if individual employees are performing to the best of their abilities. Likewise, it's just as important for employees to know where they stand and how far they have come. That's why employees need a self-measurement tool that's private, which reflects their individual ideas and thoughts without input or a set formula from management.

One way to help employees keep check of where they are and what they've accomplished is with a 90-day mailback performance improvement worksheet (see next page). A good time to introduce this personal and confidential self-measurement tool is after you've met with an employee and he or she has set specific goals for ongoing and continuous performance.

90-Day Mailback
Performance Improvement Worksheet

Instructions to employee: This worksheet will be kept confidential and for your use only. Take time to record here the personal and professional goals and performance improvement objectives you will work toward in order to develop the skills necessary for peak performance. Be specific. List action steps and dates of completion.

To help you keep on track and stay focused on your goals and objectives, this worksheet will be mailed directly back to you in three months. When you have completed this worksheet, fold and place it in a number 10 envelope, seal and then self-address, or fold the worksheet to the size of a number 10 envelope, seal with tape, or a sticker, and self-address it. Give this to your supervisor or manager who will mail this back to you in 90 days.

When you receive the mailback worksheet three months from now, take time to review the performance goals you set and determine if you are still on track. If you have accomplished everything you set out to, then you can feel good about what you have done, congratulate yourself, and continue on your performance track. If you have dropped the ball along the way, or missed any of the key areas of improvement on which you promised to work, this goal review will serve as a helpful reminder that you need to get back on track and start focusing on these areas as soon as possible. Ask for help if you need it.

Note to Manager: The effect that filling out and reviewing this performance improvement worksheet will have on your employees can be substantial. It is an honest way for someone to measure whether he or she has stayed on task in pursuit of critical performance objectives. If the aims and objectives are met, employees will gain a sense of self-satisfaction from knowing they followed through. If they are not met, no harm is done because only the employee will have seen the worksheet. It will certainly serve, however, as a hard-hitting reminder of what that person committed to yet failed to complete. You may be surprised at the positive feedback you receive after you have mailed back these worksheets. After 90 days, people tend to forget that they even completed this worksheet, and when it arrives it really can make quite an impact.

Be sure to mark your calendar for when to mail these worksheets to your people. Forgetting to do so will send a negative message that you simply do not care enough to help employees track their performance and ongoing progress.

90-DAY MAILBACK
PERFORMANCE IMPROVEMENT WORKSHEET

Name _____ **Date** _____

I will place my greatest emphasis on improving my performance in the following areas over the next 90-day period to further enhance my personal and professional development and productivity. I am listing here the action steps I will take and the date(s) by which I will accomplish them.

_____

_____

_____

_____

_____

_____

_____

Who's Keeping Score?

One of the tried and true business maxims, "What gets measured is what gets done," is just as relevant today as it ever was. No matter how creative, nontraditional, or globally directed their performance might be, organizations around the world still have to find viable ways to measure what's actually getting done in the organization. That's when the question of measurable improvement rises to the surface, and you can bet someone will be keeping score.

Throughout this book you've been given lots of fast phrases that you can use. The following is another fast tool to go with those phrases when it comes to measuring employee performance in real time, on the job. It's called an experiential follow-up assignment—with an emphasis on the word *experiential*—referring to actual on-the-job activity.

Experiential Follow-Up Assignment

This on-the-job exercise gives important and measurable feedback to managers and keeps the employee mindful of how she or he is developing in the process.

This assignment also is helpful when it is used immediately following any training session, coaching session, or meeting to implement change and higher performance standards.

Instructions to employee: This assignment will provide valuable feedback to your manager or supervisor. Be sure to turn in this completed assignment at the end of the 30-day deadline. Your specific feedback will be helpful in measuring increased performance on the job and areas of difficulty you also may be experiencing.

Respond to the following (add sheets of paper when necessary):

1. What specific performance improvements have you been able to apply on the job? What specific performance improvements have you witnessed by others? Describe them and how you measure their success.

   _____

   _____

   _____

   _____

   _____

   _____

   _____

   _____

2. Describe one or more real-world situations that you have been able to handle more effectively as a result of additional training or coaching. What was your biggest challenge at the start? How did you apply the coaching you received to produce higher performance on the job? What results have you witnessed these past 30 days?

_____
_____
_____
_____
_____
_____
_____
_____
_____

3. What tools, tips, techniques, resources, equipment, and the like have you been using on the job that, in your opinion, have measurably improved performance this past month? Could these performance levels have been achieved without this support? Explain why or why not.

_____
_____
_____
_____
_____
_____
_____
_____
_____

4. Please add your additional comments and feedback for your manager or supervisor as it pertains to improved performance on the job. Contribute your ideas for measuring performance and how you will support ongoing ways to continue peak performance and higher productivity.

_____

_____

_____

_____

_____

_____

_____

_____

Deadline: This part is important. Complete this experiential follow-up assignment and return to your manager or supervisor [name here] no later than [date here].

_____

_____

_____

Note to manager: Measuring how employees gain productive performance in real-world scenarios tells you as a leader how employees are doing day to day. It also tells you how employees are using the training they get and the lessons they learn in their jobs. This information can be extremely helpful to a manager when it comes time to justify training time and expense, equipment, and other resources requested. This tool can be used to turn them into validated investments. Remember, what gets measured is what gets done.

Tips for Documenting Performance Problems Within Teams

Many different team types exist, and most are connected with specific organizational processes or functions. Before performance problems within teams are documented, it's smart to determine the team type and the team's unique function as it relates to higher performance.

Here are a few perfect phrases for determining performance issues within certain types of teams and then documenting them:

Team-Type Phrases

High-Performing and Self-Directed Teams

- High-performing and self-directed teams means that the team itself is accountable and responsible for what's going on. If there is a problem with this type of team, it is usually because the members who are charged with doing a task have not done it well or completed it. Document who's doing what and who's holding the team back from higher performance and productivity.

Functional and Cross-Functional Teams

- Functional and cross-functional teams are made up of a group of employees who work together in one department. That group is responsible for generating output and improving functional processes in that department. If that's not happening, begin documenting who's not pulling their weight and why. List what functional processes aren't being completed. It's the job of cross-functional teams to come together from different organizational departments in an effort to share information that will improve the overall process. Is there anyone not sharing the information? Document it and find out why.

Senior Executive Teams

■ Senior executive teams are usually made up of the CEO, president, and other senior-level executives. This can be a difficult group about which to document performance issues, but someone's got to do it. If the senior executive team is not providing vision and specific goals for others to follow, that omission needs to be brought to their attention. Ask for vision and mission statements, clarification, and more specifics when this situation occurs.

Middle-Management Teams

■ Middle-management teams require bringing together managers from a variety of departments within the organization, including the director who heads them up. Their job is to ensure consistency among the workers who make up their departments and who are responsible for disseminating new policies and sharing information. If a middle manager isn't spreading the news of new policies or effectively sharing information in a timely manner, then that situation needs to be documented by someone. Usually discussing the problem with the director of the department can help to ensure that appropriate documentation is taking place.

Retooling Teams or Process Improvement Teams

■ Retooling teams or process improvement teams are usually temporary. These teams are often charged with the tasks of reengineering, or developing new processes to replace old processes. Sometimes these teams can get stuck, and new processes are not really an improvement over the old ones. If this situation occurs, it needs to be documented. If reengineering, or reorganizing a department, is at hand, then specifics of how this change is going to improve performance needs to be documented. Often these teams are cross-functional in nature, because their efforts affect many different departments or divisions within the organization. This influence makes the documentation of how processes are being improved quite important.

Project Teams

■ Project teams can be functional or cross-functional, and they are usually established on a temporary basis. These teams bring together all of the specialty areas within a company that are equipped to plan and execute a variety of special projects. Their efforts may be targeted toward the company itself or toward its customer base. It's important that teams of this sort document any performance problems as they relate to planning the project and then carrying it out. If someone is holding back the process of execution, for example, that obstacle needs to be documented and confronted immediately.

New-Product Design Teams

- New-product design teams pull together a range of workers within the organization who will be involved in the design, development, manufacturing, and rollout of any new product or service. These teams can be both temporary and permanent, and their goal is seamless delivery of new products and services. Any behaviors that would thwart seamless delivery would be cause for detailed documentation.

Virtual Teams

- Virtual teams and teammates can be spread across the planet, connecting in cyberspace and sometimes never meeting or talking face-to-face with other team members or their leaders. This unique type of team lends itself to a variety of performance issues that can occur, such as not communicating fast enough within a wide time zone difference, difficulty in understanding cultural diversity, or having a need to see people face-to-face in order to be a high-performing team player. These are all areas that should be documented when virtual teams are experiencing glitches.

When you understand the various types of teams and know what to look for when documenting a wide array of performance problems that can arise from them, you will be better equipped for selecting appropriate team members and ultimately getting the job done. The following perfect phrases and questions can be useful in the documentation process.

Eight Perfect Phrases for Creating a Dream Team of High Performance

1. Select the right people who possess the most talent for that particular team.
2. Communicate openly and honestly with all team members; document specifically what you want to convey.
3. Ask for and expect feedback in writing from team members.
4. Don't micromanage. Commit yourself to delegating decision making to the team.
5. Care about each team and its people.
6. Provide the tools and resources necessary to ensure the team's success.
7. Coach team players at their level of competence.
8. Always encourage esprit de corps!

Perfect Phrases That Use Questions for Documenting Team Performance

1. How will you handle establishing esprit de corps among team members? How will you document a lack of esprit de corps?
2. When a teammate isn't a good fit, how will you document this problem? What phrases can you use?
3. How will you document the pros and cons of leading a virtual team?
4. What are some of the problems you can document about a self-directed team that isn't performing to standard?
5. What are some of the most important performance issues at stake when it comes to a team's success? How will you document them?

6. Which team members do you think require the most support?
7. To which team members can you delegate with confidence?
8. Which team members have potential but are having performance difficulties? How can you coach their performance for the benefit of the team? Do you believe that a team can coach the performance of one its own teammates?

Moving Performance Forward

When it comes to documenting performance problems within teams, a manager must first understand the different team types and their unique set of performance requirements to do the job. Once this is established, a leader can determine the smart questions to ask for documenting team-related problems and create a variety of phrases that fit the situation at hand.

Real leadership enables others to take action. It means that, as a leader, you don't hoard the power but instead give it away, trusting that the team will compensate for their performance weaknesses and areas of inexperience.

Documenting performance problems in the most efficient way is how you can best move the team's performance forward.

Conclusion

Minding the Gap Between Performance Problems and Optimum Performance!

Abraham Lincoln once said, "I am not always bound to win, but I am bound to be true. I am not always bound to succeed, but I am bound to live up to what light I have." By today's standards, this could be the ultimate meaning of what it takes when it comes to minding the gap between the performance we seek as we encounter problems in the workplace and the optimum performance each of us has within us when given the chance to demonstrate it.

MINDING THE GAP

The term *mind the gap* is often used in Great Britain. The words *mind the gap* are actually written on the platforms of the underground, or subway system, throughout England. Sometimes a recorded voice also can be heard saying *please mind the gap* as a train approaches and the train doors open for passengers.

To mind the gap is a reminder that there is a slight crack or opening between the train platform and the train itself and, therefore, people should be mindful to watch their step as they enter the train.

Over the years, the term has gained popularity and is seen on T-shirts throughout London. It is often used by managers worldwide in reference to our mindfulness when it comes to looking out for the cracks and crevices that can trip us up as we attempt to move forward.

In this book you've been given an abundance of ways to document a myriad of problems on the job. You have also been provided a toolkit of various techniques with which you can help improve troubled performance and help sustain positive performance over time. The key is to get cooperation and buy-in from as many people as possible, hence avoiding malcontent.

The Lone Malcontent

At all costs, avoid the lone malcontent. This means you should never stop eliciting the enthusiasm and cooperation of everyone involved and not just a handful of people. Don't leave anyone out. Every person reinforces the others. A lone malcontent, or even one person who is left out of the flow of things, can drag the entire team down with his or her dissatisfaction or complaining. And even if that person doesn't impede the organization's overall success, you'll find yourself spending way too much time doing damage control. Getting everyone on board is a preventative measure that managers can implement, thus avoiding unnecessary employee dissatisfaction down the road.

Getting in Sync

As a manager, it is incumbent upon you to continually try to close the gap between the performance problems you may be experiencing and the high performance you are seeking. One way to do this is to get your departments and your people in alignment.

Doing so is more easily accomplished when everyone is in sync. Synchronization takes place when individual departments within the organization and employee expectations within those departments together support the overall mission, vision, and goals of its leadership. In other words, everyone must be moving in the same direction, for the same reason, in order to get the same results.

In Part Two of this book, we examined how The Ritz-Carlton Hotels take strategy and performance to a higher level. That was a perfect example of synchronicity and alignment in action and how both importance and performance come together when we continue to mind the gap. In the case of The Ritz-Carlton, they consider synchronicity to be so important that it is practiced on a daily basis, worldwide.

What are you doing to mind the gap in your organization when it comes to improving performance? Documenting performance problems using relevant phrases is certainly one way this is done. Another way is to gauge the alignment of people and their departments by taking the following actions (see the figure on the next page for a graphic representation of the process):

- Ask employees to describe what performance, or success, looks like in their unit or department, based on the specific goals and objectives set by leadership. Departmental priorities and expectations of people should always add up to and support the organization's overall goals.

- Decide if there are discrepancies between departmental and individual priorities. If so, work to close the gap, for more unity and better focus.

- Finally, ask how people think success should be measured. Measurements must be relative to the individuals who are charged with the responsibility for doing the job. Only those who actually do the work should be determining what success looks like and how that success is best measured.

By asking questions like these and getting people to think through this process, you will almost instantly be aligning people and departments with your organization's overall direction and performance standards. And as a bonus, you'll be creating strategic partners at all levels of the organization for ongoing higher performance and greater productivity. When this is accomplished, you'll find that the suggested phrases in this book will also align themselves more perfectly to documenting employee performance at every level and in a wide variety of circumstances. The rest is up to you.

Close the Gap by Aligning Departments and People with Overall Business Strategies
The organization's mission, vision, and goals must be clear.

This Way to Higher Levels of Performance and Productivity
Department priorities and expectations of people should add up to and support the company's overall business strategies and objectives.

Measurements must be relative to the individuals who are charged with the responsibility for doing the work. The people doing the work should determine what success looks like and how that success can be measured.
Get in Sync, Create Strategic Partners

Appendix A

Sample Performance Builder

An additional fast and easy way is available to help broaden your scope of awareness and sensitivity as a manager as you reference this book to document performance problems and measure an employee's growth and development.

Rather than continue using the same old annual performance appraisal form or document, why not consider adding another dimension to the entire effort? This isn't to suggest that you do away with the existing format for documenting and reviewing employee performance, but there's certainly no harm in improving upon it. Therefore, as a supplement to documenting performance problems, try adding on a Performance Builder.

A Performance Builder is a powerful tool that you can easily implement by following an eight-part performance-building plan. The title "Performance Builder" is self-explanatory. We can have all of the perfect phrases necessary for documenting performance problems, but if we don't back those phrases up with a way for people to build on their weaknesses and take action steps to recover from the problem, then what's the use?

The following sample Performance Builder not only helps to build people's performance in the areas in which they need help, but it also builds their confidence, communications skills, vision, understanding, and accountability. And that's what's clearly missing in most performance documentation these days. This is what's known as the third dimension of performance documentation. First comes documenting performance problems using the best phrases possible, like the ones in this book; second comes backing up those phrases with specific examples; and third comes a plan of action for actually helping that person to improve in his or her most challenging areas and then to succeed in them. It's all about continuous and ongoing improvement.

The great thing about using a Performance Builder in tandem with a performance appraisal, or review, is that it actually involves the employees in setting standards by which they will ultimately be measured. Included in this sample Performance Builder is an added bonus—a valuable Professional Development Self-Scoring Card complete with self-scoring tools to help employees discern where they have experienced measurable improvement after training, or reviews, have taken place.

How to Use the Performance Builder

As always, it's up to you, the manager, to adapt the following format and tools to your organization and departmental needs, management style, business sense, and people skills. Everything is contextual. Do not expect every technique and tool to work in every context. It won't. So adapt accordingly.

The objective of using a Performance Builder component when documenting performance issues is to help you to become better equipped to motivate others to perform at peak levels, while building a bridge between the employee's own interests and talents and the interests and talents of the organization.

Sample Performance Builder

PART 1

Start by defining what performance means to you as a leader. Never assume that your employees will know what you mean by the word *performance*. It is your responsibility as a leader to define the term as clearly as possible in the context of your organization and its unique culture. The word can take on different meanings, depending on whether you manufacture computers, sell software, market professional services, or custom-design houses. Don't make the assumption that an employee automatically knows what you mean when you say *performance*.

Take a moment to define what you mean by *performance* here:

_____

_____

_____

_____

PART 2

Together with your employee, establish clear and specific performance expectations. Invite discussion and encourage your employee to suggest his or her own parameters for measuring performance. By doing this you will be getting a good sense of what that employee believes is realistic.

117

As a leader, you are the one who must first describe the standards of performance that you expect from a particular job. Characterize what you think is outstanding performance and what you consider to be unacceptable performance. Ask your employee for his or her input on this.

Research shows time and again that when employees are involved in their own performance measurement, they are more likely to rise up and meet the challenge.

List your performance expectations here:

_____

_____

_____

_____

Add the input of your employee's expectations here:

_____

_____

_____

_____

PART 3

Avoid complacency at all costs. Stretch your employee and help her or him buy into improving performance. Employees buy into standards worthy of their time, investment, and energy. Getting employee buy-in isn't about creating a manipulative and compelling agenda. Consider performance measurement a joint venture and treat your employees like partners. When managers do so, employees are more likely to be genuinely motivated to buy into the standards set for them and stretch themselves to reach higher performance levels. Remember, most employees want to take a role in raising their own performance expectations. Why not give them the chance to do so? Why not raise the bar?

_____

_____

_____

_____

PART 4

Be explicit about the scope of responsibility you are giving to others. Be sure everyone involved understands exactly who is responsible for what. When employees understand their responsibilities in relationship to everyone else, the possibility of confusion is quickly eliminated.

Help employees to be spontaneous! Stress to each person that an employee's scope of responsibility may change at any time, depending on unforeseen circumstances that may arise. Explain that adapting to unplanned situations is part of the employee's job and that when it happens it's okay to broaden the scope of responsibility. Again, as the one in charge, you must be clear about what "broadening the scope of responsibility" means to you.

Take time to describe what this means to you here:

_____

_____

_____

_____

PART 5

Get it on paper. Document what's been agreed upon. This is a critical step in the Performance Builder. It goes hand in hand with this book's strong message on how to go about effectively finding perfect phrases for documenting performance problems. Create a written list of all the performance standards upon which you and your employee have agreed. Know that this will not be enough to guide your employee to achieving success. It's important for you to be specific about what it's going to actually take to reach those expectations and attain those goals—step by step.

Here is a good place to document those steps so that they can serve as your employee's course of action.

List Performance Standards	What's It Going to Make It Happen?

Important note: Give a copy of what's been agreed upon to your employee and keep the original document in your file. Later, if you are faced with the task of selecting phrases to document a performance problem, this exercise will serve you well as the platform from which mutual agreement was reached when setting acceptable standards of performance.

PART 6

Follow up as you go. It is essential that you make the time to observe and follow up with your employees on how things are going. Don't wait until the next review, or the last minute, to check in to see how things are going. Always observe and give feedback on jobs in progress. With your less-experienced employees you might have to check in more often until they feel comfortable with their responsibilities.

Describe here when and how you are going to follow up:

_____

_____

_____

_____

PART 7

Offer recognition and rewards, and don't forget to keep your promises. Be clear up front with an employee when a Performance Builder is being completed. Explain what can be expected if someone meets or exceeds the goals set. (Examples of rewards might be money; more responsibility; special recognition, such as an award certificate; a day off; a two-hour lunch break; or a more flexible work schedule.) Build in lots of small wins along the way too. Make recognition a part of the plan. Demonstrate how rewards and behaviors connect. And never make a promise without a plan to keep it. Broken promises destroy credibility.

List examples of the rewards and recognition you might give someone:

_____

_____

_____

_____

PART 8

Provide employees with the necessary professional development and training resources to be successful. It is said that one of the secrets to IBM's early success was that the organization trained and trained. When it comes to performance-building techniques, training and employee development should be at the top of your mind. Focus training on employees' needs. Ask employees what they need to learn—they will tell you! Don't arbitrarily decide that for them. And be sure to deliver training "just in time." This means getting training to people as close as possible to the time they really need it.

List questions you might ask employees regarding needed training and resources:

_____

_____

_____

_____

Measuring the Value of Professional Development and Training

Give your employees the tools they need that will bolster their confidence and contribute valuable feedback to the organization regarding its investment in professional development and training. In other words, give employees a tool to score themselves and quickly measure how far they have come in a specific learning process. Keep in mind that most people will be much harder on themselves when grading their performance than anyone else might be when measuring that same performance effort.

How to Use the Professional Development Self-Scoring Card

Use the following tool as a template to help employees self-measure ongoing improvement. Be flexible. Feel free to change and alter topics, or areas of improvement to be measured, when you feel it is necessary. Note that using figures to score a skill area is acceptable because it is a reflection on the performance skill and not on the person. Using figures to grade a person's ability is not the most desirable way to measure performance, as was discussed early on in this book.

Furthermore, using figures in this example works because employees score themselves. Using numbers on a scale of 1 to 10 makes it easy to quickly assess measurable improvement in percentages. When you are able to offer upper-level management percentages of self-improvement, assigning a dollar value to the significance of the performance improvement is far easier to do, as is tracking return on investment.

Professional Development Self-Scoring Card Template

This Professional Development Self-Scoring Card should be used as a template to quickly and easily measure individual development and improvement in specific areas of performance. The Self-Scoring Card is designed to be a useful tool to gauge growth and identify areas in which additional improvement and development may be required. The best part is, your employees are the ones doing the grading.

The number 1 is lowest in rating and the number 10 is highest in rating.

PERFORMANCE AREA	My Grade Prior	My Grade After	% Measurable Improvement
Sample: Listening Skills	7	10	30%
Coaching Others			
Project Management			
Safety			
Technical Skill Development			
Personal Growth			
Goal Setting			
Conflict Resolution			
Written Communication			
Meeting Deadlines			
Customer Care			
Decision Making			
Punctuality			
Attitude			
Appearance			
Negotiation Skills			

Note: It is recognized that there are variations in percentages using tens. This formula is rounded off to the nearest full percentage point for ease of use and flexibility.

Perfect Phrases Follow-Up Checklist on Performance Building When Used in Conjunction with Performance Appraisal

Use this helpful checklist to review the eight critical Performance Builder steps to be taken. Again, don't forget to adapt, add on, or reassign matters of importance, depending on your company's specific needs and the needs of your department or team.

- ☑ Define what *performance* means to you as a leader.

- ☑ Together with your employees, establish clear and specific performance expectations.

- ☑ Stretch employees and help them buy into improving performance.

- ☑ Be clear about the scope of responsibility you are giving.

- ☑ Document what's been agreed upon.

- ☑ Follow up.

- ☑ Offer recognition and rewards. Keep your promises.

- ☑ Provide your employees with the necessary training and resources to be successful.

Always expect the best from people. Chances are good that that is what you will get.

Appendix B

Problem-Solving Toolkit to Raise Perfect Phrases

Sometimes the perfect phrase can be a question.

This is a fast and easy-to-use 12-part toolkit, which will help guide you to examining and correcting problems facing your department, team, or organization. The process uses basic phrases and questions that, when posed to employees, often bring to the surface the real performance issue at hand and, therefore, the perfect phrase and the perfect solution that goes with it!

Define a performance challenge or problem that you may find yourself facing, such as, Do my employees really have the training or knowledge to do the job right? Is there a better process than the one we are using now? Are my employees facing obstacles of which I am unaware?

Once you've identified your employees' problems, select the most appropriate phrases or questions from this toolkit to help further uncover a troubling issue and, thereby, get to the bottom of matters. Let these phrases and questions further help you to analyze the underlying problem that may be at hand. As a result, you'll waste less time. Remember, smart managers don't presume to have all the answers. Instead, they ask smart questions and use perfect phrases for documenting performance problems.

1. Stop wasting time. Get to the heart of the matter.
   Be direct. Start by asking, What is the problem?
   a. What is the difference between what is being done and what is expected?
   b. Describe your proof.
   c. How reliable is your proof?

2. Performance discrepancies.
   a. Are they important? How so?
   b. What happens if we do nothing?
   c. Is it even worth taking time to make the problem better?

3. Performance problems because of lack of skill.
   a. Could the performers do the job if their lives depended on doing it correctly?
   b. Evaluate skills. Are they even adequate, or are they below adequate?

4. Evaluating past performance.
   a. Has past performance been better? When?
      What were the commonalities?
   b. Have current employees forgotten what they were trained to do?
   c. Do people still know what is expected of them?

5. Mastering skills by using them frequently.
   a. Do employees get regular feedback on how they are doing?
   b. How is the way people are doing communicated to them?
   c. Do employees like the way in which they are provided feedback?

6. Better ways to do things.
   a. Is there another process that will get the job done?
   b. Would a better job description be useful?
   c. Can employees relearn the task by watching others?
   d. Can the process be changed or improved in some way?

7. Having what it takes to be successful at doing the job.
   a. What does it take to do the job successfully?
   b. Is the physical and/or mental potential of the people involved strong enough?
   c. Are people truly qualified?

8. Performance and punishment.
   a. Is performance being punished?
   b. What is in it for the person to do it right?
   c. Is doing the job somehow self-punishing?
   d. Is there a reason not to perform well?

9. When not doing the job gets rewarded.
   a. Have there been rewards in the past for doing it wrong?
   b. Does doing it wrong draw attention to the person?

    c. Do employees worry less, have less anxiety and tension, or get less tired if they do less work?

10. Doing it right matters.
    a. Is there a favorable outcome for doing it right?
    b. Are there consequences for not doing it right?
    c. Is there pride in doing the job?
    d. Is there any status or lack of it connected with the job?

11. Obstacles to high performance.
    a. Do employees know what is expected of them?
    b. Do employees know when it is expected?
    c. Is competition making it too difficult?
    d. Are time and tools available?
    e. Is the job physically a mess and disorganized?

12. Limitations on possible solutions.
    a. Are there solutions that would be considered unacceptable to the organization?
    b. Do leaders have preferred solutions? Are those leaders open to suggestions for improvement by workers?
    c. Can the organization afford the time and resources to find real solutions to real problems?

Once you've practiced using this toolkit, you will likely find the technique to be a fast and easy one and something that you'll refer to again and again on the job.

About the Author

Over the years, **Anne Bruce** has evolved from the best-selling author of several books in the field of human behavior and performance, customer service, leadership, and motivation, to an inspirational force and specialist in human development and personal growth.

In her book, *Discover True North* (McGraw-Hill, 2004), Anne passionately demonstrates, with nuts-and-bolts transformation, the tools and techniques necessary to build on our signature strengths. Other bestselling books by Anne include *Motivating Employees* (McGraw-Hill), *Building a High Morale Workplace*, (McGraw-Hill), *Leaders—Start to Finish: A Road Map for Developing and Training Leaders at All Levels* (ASTD Publishing), and *Motivating Every Employee: 24 Proven Tactics to Spark Creativity in the Workplace* (McGraw-Hill).

Anne has appeared on the *CBS Evening News with Dan Rather*, the *Charlie Rose Show*, and *Good Morning America*, and has been interviewed in *USA Today*, the *London Times*, the *Wall Street Journal*, and the *Boston Globe*. Anne has been a featured speaker for The White House, Coca-Cola, Sprint, Ben & Jerry's, Blue Cross/Blue Shield, Southwest Airlines, JetBlue, and the Conference Board of Europe. Anne also hosts her own radio talk show called *Anne Bruce Life Coach*. She has instructed programs at both Harvard and Stanford Law Schools.

For more information on workshops and keynote speeches associated with this book and others, visit Anne's Web site at www.annebruce.com. You also can e-mail her at anne@annebruce.com, or call 214-507-8242. Anne is well known for her high-energy and extremely entertaining and engaging training events, as well as for her award-winning platform speeches to multinational organizations worldwide.